The Legendary Lost To

On the trail of Yorkshire's famou...

Phil Mathison

Published by Dead Good Publications
Newport,
East Yorkshire
HU15 2RF

© 2015

Front cover
Aerial view of Spurn Point, taken in the early 1990s at the time of a very low spring tide. The black patch just north of the lighthouse on the river side is the Old Den. Just above that on the seaward side, can be seen a light coloured trail heading north east out under the waves. I believe that this is the last vestige of the peninsula in the time of Ravenser Odd.

Rear cover
The Kilnsea cross, which is reputed to have come from Ravenspurn. Apparently it was placed there to commemorate the landing of Henry, Duke of Lancaster in 1399. Drawing by John Child in 1818, just before the cross was dismantled and removed to Burton Constable

OTHER TITLES BY THE AUTHOR

Shed Bashing with the The Beatles (ISBN 9780954693732)
The Spurn Gravel Trade (ISBN 9780954693763)
The Saint of Spurn Point (ISBN 9780956299406)
Tolkien in East Yorkshire 1917-18, An Illustrated Tour (ISBN 9780956299413)
On Macabre Lines, Original railway tales to haunt the imagination (ISBN 9780956299420)

ISBN 978-0-9562994-3-7

Published by Dead Good Publications
Newport,
East Yorkshire
HU15 2RF

Contents

Foreword

My fascination with the lost town of Ravenser Odd began in 1995, when I 'rediscovered' Spurn Point, the peninsula at the very south eastern corner of Yorkshire, after many years during which this interesting location had never entered my thoughts. Once re-awakened, my passion for the promontory led me to devour as many books as possible on the area. Tales of a vanished port soon came to light, and so for nearly twenty years I have gathered information on this legendary place.

The book is effectively composed of two parts – an overview of the main historical facts about Ravenser, and the subsequent detective work that I have undertaken to ascertain what became of the town, and where exactly it was. For those readers unfamiliar with the topic, this slim volume will give a clear introductory insight into the main body of information on the town. Readers who are more knowledgeable will find much that is familiar to them, but there is also some new information. I believe that the chapters on the fate of the town and its location will be read with keen interest by all who have a fascination with the place. To those in both groups of reader who want to take their interest further, I can do no better than to direct them to the main texts listed in the bibliography, many very well known indeed.

However, there they will find a new title listed – Molly Tatchell : Ravenser Odd, Lost Port of the Humber. This amazing discovery came about when I went across to Grimsby Library in the spring of 2008, to further my research on Spurn Point. I immediately had a copy made, and ensured that an additional copy was sent to the Hull Local History Library. Molly, who died in 2003, was from Cleethorpes and worked at the Public Record Office in London. She obviously spent years unearthing all that she could about Ravenser, and then, as a labour of love, she typed it all up and sent a copy to the library at Grimsby. Her letter to Mr J H Mayor, then senior librarian at the Central Library in the town, dated March 9th 1994, ends with the wonderfully prophetic sentence – 'I am pleased to think that my book may be of use to local historians.' Indeed it has been, and Molly is to be thanked and praised for all her work in producing the text. If any of Molly Tatchell's relatives chance upon this volume, please contact me, as I would dearly love to thank them for her unselfish efforts, and to communicate further with them.

As always, this book would not have been possible without the assistance of a number of people. First must be my wife, Mary, who has had to endure years of my ramblings, both verbal and actual, on this topic, and has the unenviable task of proof reading my deliberations. No book on Spurn Point would be complete without acknowledgement of the author's indebtedness to the late George De Boer. His work has been seminal to the understanding of this fascinating place. Thanks are also due to George De Boer's estate for permission to use the diagram of his cyclical theory of Spurn over the centuries.

Two people who are the cornerstones of any study of Spurn Point are next. Jan Crowther has always been a fount of knowledge on the area, and willing to share any resources that she has in the furtherance of understanding the history of Yorkshire's extreme peninsula. Next is Andy Gibson, who has spent many years working for the Yorkshire Wildlife Trust, first at the Spurn nature reserve, and latterly, covering much of the Humber area generally. Andy has an incisive mind that makes me question and re-examine any research that I have done. Barbara English of Hull University kindly read over the text of Molly Tatchell's work and gave comments and advice. I must also mention Harry Watkins, and Andy Mason, both who have served as heritage officers for YWT, and have shared and encouraged my passion for this particular historical research. I'd like to thank Anna Maria Dutto for creating the line maps of my hypothetical evolution of the peninsula between 1066 and 1620. The staff at Beverley Treasure House have as always, been patient and extremely helpful on my numerous visits to this well stocked archive. The Hull History Centre has likewise proved invaluable at many points in my research. Finally, I must mention Jennie Mooney at Grimsby Library, who has always risen to the challenge of supplying me with the photocopies and information that I have requested. If I have missed anyone else out, trust me, any help with my research, no matter how small, has been greatly appreciated, and I hope that the end result presented here is some small recompense for any input I have received from many people over the years.

Phil Mathison

August 2015

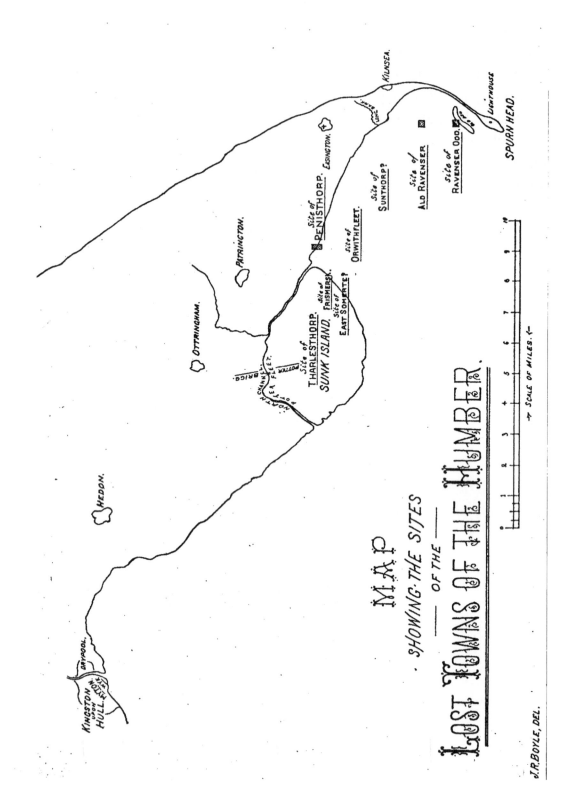

MAP

SHOWING THE SITES

OF THE

LOST TOWNS OF THE HUMBER.

J.R. BOYLE, DEL.

SCALE OF MILES.

Introduction to Ravenser

To start the remarkable tale of this remarkable town, we must first clarify where exactly we are talking about. It was a town, or rather towns, with a serious identity crisis, for there were ultimately four places that could lay some claim to the title of Ravenser. The taxation roll of 1297 lists three places as Ravenser, Old Ravenser and Odd. To these three, we could ultimately add Ravenserspurn. For the time being I am ignoring any references to an earlier location called Hrafnseyr (the raven tongue of land) mentioned when Harold drove the Norsemen from England after the Battle of Stamford Bridge in 1066. I will return to the matter of Hrafnseyr and Ravenserspurn later in the book.

Before this significant port came into being c1230 A.D., there was a hamlet called Ravenser, south of Kilnsea in the furthest extremity of Holderness. It was of little consequence, having a manor house and very few dwelling places. No great volume of trade or activity are recorded as having taken place there, and it was quickly overshadowed by the commercial centre that grew a mile away and became known as Ravenser Odd. This new site had a variety of names and spellings. For example, I have discovered these various names and spellings for the town; Ravensrode, Od or Odd, Od near Ravenser, Ravenesodd, Ravenesher, Ravenserot, Ravensroad, Ravensrodde, Ravensredde, le Hod, Ravenserhod, Odrauenser, Hodde, Raueneshereodde, and this list may not be exhaustive. The original hamlet then became known as Ald, Auld, or Old Ravenser. Below we read how an ancient chronicler attempted to clarify the matter.

'That the distinction between the two towns may be known (it may be mentioned that) the former Ravenserre, where now nothing remains except a single manor-house with its appurtenances, and which is inland, and distant both from the sea and the Humber, is called Ald Ravenser, and this by the people of to-day, although the other town is altogether consumed. But that town of Ravenserre Odd, at one time commonly called Odd near Ravensere, and afterwards (simply) Ravensere, occupying a position in the utmost limits of Holderness, between the waters of the sea and those of the Humber, was distant from the main land (a firma terra) a space of one mile and more. For access to which from ancient time from Ald Ravensere, a sandy road extended, covered with round and yellow stones, thrown up in a little time by the height of the floods, having a breadth which an archer can scarcely shoot across, and wonderfully maintained by the tides of the sea on its east side, and the ebb and flow of the Humber on its west side. Which road remains visible both to pedestrian and equestrian travellers; but its furthest part, for the space of half a mile, has been washed into the Humber since those days by the tides of the sea. Of the site therefore of the said town of Ravensere Odd scarcely a vestige remains. Which town, belonging to the parish of the church of Esyngton, was distant from the town of Esyngton about four miles. Between which towns of Esyngton and Odd, the town of Kylnse and the town of Sunthorpe and the manor of Ald Ravensere in the parish of the church of Kynlnse are known lie midway.' (LTH p11, from CM ii p30 and CM p121 - 122)

The new town of Ravenser Odd rapidly grew and flourished, and then, like some spectacular shooting star, burnt out and disappeared, all in the space of about 130 years. The town had ceased to exist by 1370. There is then little reference to the place until 1399, when suddenly Ravensburg, Ravenspur, or Ravnespurne appear in the records. Was this new name appertaining to the location of the lost port, or was it to be found on a new sandbank in the vicinity? I will attempt to shed light on this matter in the subsequent pages.

The main thrust of my narrative will concern the new town of Ravenser Odd, for new town it was. In the 12th and 13th centuries, many new towns were seeded in England, for it was the desire of the ruling classes that these centres should generate wealth and trade in the land. They would become new sources of taxation and revenue, for such thoughts were always present in the lords' minds. Additionally, their markets would provide food and sustenance for the lords' servants and tenants, and raw materials for use in their manors. Ravenser Odd, Hedon, Wyke (Hull) and Skipsea were all new towns in the area (NTMA p78). Some, like Hull and Hedon prospered, but Skipsea failed. Ravenser Odd prospered exceptionally well until the sea claimed it, and the silting of the Haven at Hedon stifled its long term prospects.

According to legend, for there is no verification about the matter, someone called 'Peter Atte See' decided to lodge in the remains of a wrecked boat stranded on the beach sometime in the 1230s. That there was a wrecked boat there at this time, we certainly do know. A plea roll dated 1231 exists in the Hull archives that states 'A certain boat was found at Ravenese and another Diminton and the bailiffs of the earl of Albemarle took them without view of the coroner, therefore to judgement concerning the earl…' (UDCC / 2 / 5). It looks as though the earl was keen to acquire these boats. Probably the development of a new town on the promontory was already forming in the earl's mind. Furthermore, this story suggests that Peter then began to sell food and drink to passing sailors, and before long, others joined him to trade on this spit. Here we are on firmer ground, for certain men of Grimsby, at an inquisition in 1290 stated;

'Asked during what period had men lived at Ravenserod, they say that forty years ago a certain ship was cast away on Ravenserod, where there was no house then built, which ship a certain person appropriated to himself, and from it made for himself a cabin (scala sive casa) which he inhabited for some time, that there he received ships and merchants and sold them meat and drink, and afterwards began to dwell there.' (LTH p16, Chancery Inquisition, 18 Edward I, No 145)

To verify that the town was on a place cast up by the sea, we can do no better than quote from actual records of the 13th century;

'That forty years ago and more (that is, about or before 1235) by the casting up of the sea, sand and stones accumulated, on which accumulation William de Fortibus, then earl of Albemarl, began to build a certain town which is called Ravenesodd; and it is an island; the sea surrounds it.' (LTH p10, Rotuli Hundredorum i, p292, 402)

So the story began; the tenuous grip by a few brave men on an outcrop; an earl keen to develop a new town under his jurisdiction, and merchants ready to capitalise on this opportunity. The town grew rapidly in the 1240s, behaving as if it were already a borough, but not actually being granted that status, along with Hull, until 1299. Its main trade was in fish, principally herring, which were very plentiful at the time, and the curing thereof. Other goods figure in the port's commerce, such as Yorkshire's staple export of the time – wool, which attracted the most tax. The first thirty years of the 14th century were the zenith of the town's short existence, with ships being supplied to the king on a number of occasions to assist in the wars with Scotland.

But mightier forces than the rebellious Scots were at hand, for from 1334 Ravenser experienced inundations from the sea and the Humber. By the 1340s, the town's fortunes were in rapid decline, and such were the depredations, that relief from taxation was being sought by 1346. The next decade brought further woe, for the churchyard was washed away, and the exposed bodies had to be reburied at Easington church. The remaining folks of this once proud town gathered up their belongings, and left for Hull or Grimsby. The last reported trade in the town was in 1358. (SH p83, CPR 1358 – 1361, 91) It was all over for the Odd by 1362, when the last human activity of any kind in the town was noted.

The substance of what we know about Ravenser has been handed down to us from two main sources – the church and the state. Meaux abbey owned land at Ravenser, and Thomas Burton, the abbot between 1396 and 1399, not long after the loss of the town, recorded in the early

15th century its ultimate fate for posterity. His deliberations are noted in the Chronicles of Meaux. Having dealt with the ecclesiastical, we now turn to the worldly. Any transaction between individuals produces records – of taxation, dealings in land, sales and purchases, trade, even of punishment. Fortunately, the state has ensured that many rolls have survived. They include the Calendar of Close Rolls, the Calendar of Patent Rolls and the Calendar of Inquisitions. Additionally, there are various documents surviving in archives such as the Hull History Centre.

It is not my intention in this work to slavishly reference everything back to these primary sources. There are references, but usually only to the books already published that anyone can access if they want to. Any references are included in parenthesis within the actual body of the text, as I find it distracting having to move back and forth between my current page and sources listed at the rear of books. I will not be taxing the reader's patience by dwelling on all the known minute details of the location, but rather to give a broad overview of the available data. It is in the revelations of the fate and location of the town that I will be forensically picking through the surviving evidence and presenting my case.

I have abbreviated references to the books used regularly in the text by giving them the following codes;

GP – George Poulson, History and Antiquities of the Seigniory of Holderness
IECS – Institute of Estuarine and Coastal Studies 1992
LH – Barbara English, The Lords of Holderness
LTH – J R Boyle, Lost towns of the Humber
LTOTYC – Thomas Sheppard, Lost towns of the Yorkshire Coast
NTMA – Maurice Beresford, New Towns of the Middle Ages
OP – Thomas Thompson, Occellum Promontorium
RO – Molly Tatchell, Ravenser Odd, Lost Port of the Humber

ROLEYT – Barbara English, Ravenser Odd, a lost East Yorkshire Town (in D B Lewis – The Yorkshire Coast)
SH – George De Boer, Spurn Head: Its History and Evolution
SOH – William Shelford; On the outfall of the river Humber
TGH – T H Lloyd, England and the German Hanse
THT – Helen Zimmern, The Hansa Towns
VCH – Victoria County History

Additionally, I have abbreviated the titles of the primary documents referenced;
CCR = Calendar of Close Rolls
CPR = Calendar of Patent Rolls
CM = The Chronicles of Melsa (Meaux)
PRO = Public Record Office
YAS = Yorkshire Archaeological Society

Historical Overview

The earliest extant record of Ravenser Odd appears in a Pipe Roll dated 1230 A.D., when the names of Matthias de Ravenser, and Odo de Ravenser appear. (SH p82, Pipe Rolls, 14 Henry III, N.S. 4, 276). Are these the first inhabitants, or was our legendary 'Peter Atte See' already there? By the next decade, the third William de Fortibus, the earl of Albemarle, was keenly interested in the town, for the Meaux Chronicle records;

'Stephen de Thorpe, knight, gave unto us (Meaux Abbey) a yearly rent of one mark out of a carucate of land in Ravenserre, which Alan Barell and his sons held in villanage. And the third William de Fortibus, earl of Albemarl, gave us a place with appurtenances, containing half an acre of land in the borough of Odd near Ravenserre; that there we might be able, as we wished, to construct for ourselves buildings suitable for our store both of herrings and other kinds of fish, in order to provide, as often as and whenever we wished, fish and other necessaries for our own use. And besides he confirmed to us the aforesaid rent of one mark in Ald Ravenser; and freed us for ever from all service and exaction, toll, tax, action at law, and other usages pertaining to the said land in Odd according to the usage of a burgage' (LTH p11, CM ii p29).

The foundations of the fishery trade were thus laid. The spawning grounds of the 'silver darlings' could decide the fate of nations, for herring fishing was to become a branch of industry. A change in the course at spawning in the 12th century gave power to Denmark in the time of Waldemar the Great (1157 – 1182). (THT p49) The main fishing period was late summer, July to September, but the Norwegians brought fish across at other times, sharing the trade with the Germans. (TGH p40) Fish was a staple food of the populace, especially in Lent. In preserved form, it was known as stockfish, and Odd had sheds for the curing of fish. To transport it, salt was required to preserve it, and it is therefore no surprise to find that salt is one of the commodities traded at Ravenser. It was not uncommon for peoples of marshland areas similar to Holderness at that time to develop the salt extraction industry. 'The type of town that salt production encouraged was a port for transhipment since the customers were scattered all over England and beyond.' (NTMA p78) Lincolnshire certainly took part in the industry, but I have found no evidence in texts that south Holderness undertook this activity. However, having examined an Ordnance Survey map of the area c1900, there are several 'saltings' listed, one near Black Moor House at Kilnsea, another near Firtholme Clough, Easington and one at Oxlands Bank, Skeffling. This would suggest that there is a probability that the salt marshes of the Humber bank did provide Ravenser with salt for its preserved fish. Additionally, salt production would augment the seigneur's revenues by its sale and the tolls levied on others upon its marketing and shipping elsewhere. Furthermore, salted herrings were an acknowledged form of tax or tribute, and even used as a medium of exchange for inland produce. (THT p27) No wonder that this safe haven, so close to the fishing grounds, prospered with such a valuable resource within easy reach of its fleet, and why the earl was so keen for its advancement.

The earl of Albemarle managed to claim successfully that he owned the site, and much to the chagrin of some of its neighbours, his new town, Ravenser Odd, behaved as though it were a borough, with all the rights that implied – a town with a mayor, burgesses, a court of its own, and various privileges of townsmen, such as being able to inherit, lease and sell their houses. (ROLEYT p150) On February 22nd 1250 -51, King Henry III granted William de Fortibus a charter allowing the town 'to hold a weekly market on Thursdays and a yearly fair lasting sixteen days, starting on September 8th, the vigil of the Nativity of the Blessed Mary, except that market and fair shall be to the injury of neighbouring markets and fairs.' (LTH p12, Rotuli Chartarum, anno 35 Hen. III., m. 12)

Somehow, the port withstood the great storm of 1253, (Hull & East Riding Portfolio Vol 3, p75) but was probably an island after that date, with the causeway often over-washed by high tides.

With the inducements listed above, it was no wonder that, storm or no storm, Ravenser Odd rapidly expanded as a 'new town'. But what did the status of a 'new town' mean? In this case, the local lord had given a piece of land to one or more local knights. He might have provided grants for building materials, which was not unusual, and he certainly obtained a charter from the king to enable townsmen to be freed of agricultural taxes. In the case of Ravenser Odd, he also gained ready access to luxury goods such as French wine, which is recorded as an import. To get some idea of the growth of the port, we only have to look at the records of the rents, called burgage, paid to the bishops. In 1260 they were £6 per annum, 1270 £12, 1271 £26, 1277 £39, 1281 £48 and 1307 £68. (NTMA p62) The Burgage rate was one shilling per burgage occupied, and each of these were only a fraction of an acre.

New towns of the era were built on a grid system like a chess board, creating a rectangular street plan. Each square in the pattern was called a chequer, and a building plot within one was called a placea. There was no standard size for placea, and there would be a number of such plots within each chequer. It was normal to pay burgage on the empty plot, no extra was paid if it was built upon, or if more buildings were added, as long as the burgess met the cost of construction himself. A whole chequer was normally assigned for the church, and one for the market place. The burgage plots would concentrate around the market hall, and many of the streets would lead off in all directions from it. (NTMA p147 – 163) It is reasonable to deduce that Ravenser Odd, like the other local new towns of Hull and Hedon, was constructed on these lines. Private residences would be away from commercial activity, for contrary to what you might think, planning laws were quite advanced. The warehouses would be next to the quay, with fish curing in the same vicinity. Any tanneries or other undesirable trades would likewise be separated from dwelling houses. We know that Odd had tanneries, as rent from them was paid to the countess of Aumale in the 1260s. (LH p212) It also possessed its own windmill, (RO p8, YAS Vol 12 p81) and the king retained a prison and a gallows in the town. (VCH Vol 5 p72, CCR 1296 – 1302, p509)

Above all, this new town was a trading port, and one with a safe anchorage, so it is no surprise to learn that the right to charge wharfage on merchandise there was given in 1296. (OP p145) Safe anchorage was vital in winter, as it was dangerous for the boats of the time, mostly 'cogges', to venture far out to sea. (THT p18) Many were under two hundred tons, and less than a hundred feet long. After Scarborough, there was no safe haven until ships could shelter in the lee of the Humber. For this purpose, Ravenser Odd was ideal. Henry III, in 1256, gave a charter to the burgesses of Scarborough by which he engaged that no port or quay should be made between that town and Ravenser. (OP p132, Hinderwell's History of Scarborough, p112) As it was considered unsafe for ships to set sail to the continent after November 11th (Martinmas), owners ideally wanted them berthed by the end of September, (Michaelmas) to avoid the worst of the storms that claimed many boats and lives. They would then stay in port until at least February 2nd (Candlemas). Ships were valuable assets for owners to lose, and so Odd during these stormy months would have been a strange sight, with a legion of masts rising above the town's roofs. It would appear that only herrings (prized for fasting) and beer were transported during this riskier season.

No account of this period can overlook the part played by the Hanseatic League. They were a guild of traders, centred on Lubeck, who controlled much of the trade in Northern Europe in the Middle Ages. Their merchants often formed enclaves within trading towns abroad, and they undertook a significant proportion of the trade at Ravenser Odd. In the years 1304 to 1309, the port handled the following Hanseatic ships: 1 in and out, 28 in only and two out only. To give an idea with regards to other ports, Hull managed 20 in and out, 20 in only and 11 out only in the same period. (TGH p42) The Germans were actively involved in the wool trade from 1270 onwards, when an Anglo-Flemish dispute boosted the trade. Also, the Anglo-French wars after 1294 further encouraged this activity. At the time, Hull and Ravenser were serious competitors to Boston and Lynn for the trade. (TGH p39) However, their part in this trade at the port had ceased by the 1320s, probably due to competition from Boston. The Hanseatics had a hand in the shipping of fish and train oil (whale oil), a trade which they shared with the Norwegians. Additionally, they were involved in the transhipment of timber, and artefacts made of timber, from the Baltic to Ravenser Odd. (TGH p42) Some corn was handled, but it was not a regular commodity. There is note of a Ravenser man in 1316 loading rye and barley in a Lubeck ship at Alborg in Denmark (TGH p49, PRO SC3 / 34 / 62), but this seems to be the exception rather than the rule. A writ to the countess of Albemarle exists from 1265 concerning a certain ship and merchandise detained at Odd. The vessel was owned by Henry Pank of Hull and had travelled from Newcastle. It had been held by William de la Twyer, her bailiff for Holderness, because amongst its cargo were swords and armour of a certain German. The instruction was for the ship and the weapons to be released, on condition that the owners, Thomas Thorald and his brother Ralph guaranteed that they would not be sold outside the kingdom. (UDCC / 2 / 9)

After the third earl died at Amiens in 1260, his widow, countess Isabella de Fortibus acquired his estates in the region, including all the lands and tenements of Ravenser. (LTH p12, UDCC / 2 / 8) Upon her death in 1293, with no surviving issue, for her daughter, Aveline, had died in 1274, the seigniory reverted to the crown and was the king's property when he made Odd a free borough in 1299. (LTH p50)

In the year 1286, a grant of assize was made to the merchants of Ravenser Odd for the exclusive right of selling bread and beer in the town. This may have been prompted by a certain Hervey Raver of Ely being granted safe conduct to sell ale as far away as the town the previous year (RO p23, CPR 1281 – 1292 p164) Here is the translation of the grant of assize mentioned above;

'The king to all to whom, etc. saluting. Because we learn by an inquisition which we have caused to be made by our beloved and faithful Thomas de N. our escheator beyond the Trent, that our people the merchants of Ravenserod are well and sufficiently able to supply in every period of the year to all and everyone resorting to that town, good bread and good beer, according to our assize therein provided, and this they are ready to do, and in nothing to fail; and that strangers, not residing in the aforesaid town of Ravenserod, influenced by cupidity, bring bread and beer in ships to be sold there, to the injury of those our people and merchants, and the great deterioration of their estate and that of the town aforesaid, and against the usage of towns so situated on the sea: We wishing to provide for the indemnity of our people and merchants in this matter, grant to them, that no stranger shall presume to sell bread or beer in the port or in the sea near the aforesaid town of Ravenserod against the will of the people our merchants aforesaid; and therefore we command you that, so far as in you lies, you do not permit anything to be done against the will of the people and merchants aforesaid. Teste Rege.'
(LTH p13 & 14, OP p138 - 139; from Hargrave's Law Tracts, i, p79)

We now have a picture of a rapidly expanding town, on the limited space available on what can only be described as an island (OP p140). The main trade was in fish, and the main export wool. Fortunes were being made, and one family, the De la Poles, was to rise to great fame and fortune. Indeed, William De la Pole amassed sufficient riches to lend a vast sum to King Edward III, and in return he was given the great manor at Burstwick. (OP p237) Ravenser Odd was a desirable place to have property, and to do business in. This did not escape the notice of the religious authorities, for in addition to Meaux abbey, Swine nunnery is noted as owning property yielding six marks, and St. Leonard's hospital at York had vacant ground worth three shillings per annum. (OP p154) Thornton abbey also had a stake in the town, for in 1300, the abbey had a certain place with appurtenances in Ravenserodd, described as follows; 'They say also that it contains in breadth 89 feet and also in length from the way which is called Newgate to the south it contains towards the Humber 240 feet and further towards the north as much as can be acquired upon the river saving the common way which leads to the "kaye". Worth 1 mark by the year only.' (UDCC / 2 / 32) The same source also mentions the streets of Kirk Lane, the common lane and Hull Street. The only other street name that we know of is a certain vacant place in 1336 called Locksmith Lane. (OP p270, LTOTYC p91) Fish was not the only trade, for timber, skins, salt, oil, pitch, wool and wine are also mentioned in the customs accounts of the early 14th century. The volume of shipping can be judged from the customs officers accounts, for in the year 1304 – 05, 118 ships are recorded as calling at the port. In the following year, 1305 – 06, 120 are noted, and in 1307 – 08, no less than 133 ships were dealt with by the customs authorities. (VCH Vol 5 p71). This may not sound a large number, but these totals would not include the fishing boats based at the port. That is because customs records do not list vessels that do not trade with other ports. Fishing craft were considered to be employed 'within the port authority's area', that is, not landing at other ports during their time fishing, and usually returning within the day. Therefore, we can assume that many of the ships at the quay were locally registered craft involved in the port's predominant trade of fish.

One notable item of trade was that in hawks, mostly from Norway. In 1271 Henry de Lacy was granted power to take goshawks, gerfalcons and falcons to the towns of Lynn, Grimsby and Ravenser Odd. In 1276 there was a writ of aid granted to William Franckes of Grimsby to buy and take to the king's use gerfalcons and falcons bought in his home port and Ravenser Odd and Hull. (RO p23) This trade obviously continued into the 14th century, for William de Ros of Hamelak was commissioned by the king in 1316 to purchase six falcons at Hull, Odd and Lynn. (RO p27, CPR 1313 – 1317 p551)

An unusual instruction was received by the administrators of town in 1300, concerning the control of coinage. (RO p24, CCR 1296 – 1302 p391) It seems that 'pollards and crockards', base metal coins used by Flemish merchants to pay for English wool, were in common circulation, and this was detrimental to trade. Therefore, it was prohibited for silver coinage to leave the kingdom, without the king's special licence. From this date, only this money could be used in the realm. Despite this injunction, it would appear that coinage was sometimes smuggled out, hidden in the sacks of wool. A French ship, driven into the port through stress of wind and sea, was found to contain £102 worth of pollards, crockards and silver items, owned by John Case of St. Omer. The money was returned to John, but only after it was converted into official currency. (RO p25, CCR 1296 – 1302 p434)

Ravenser Odd became a place to do business, and it is therefore perhaps not surprising that sometimes the spirit of laissez faire went too far. It was alleged in 1313 that the burgesses of the port usurped the king's rights by hindering his officers and forfeiting goods and customs payments. (VCH Vol 5 p72, CPR 1313 – 1317, 273 & 582) Sometimes the desire to take the law into their own hands led the merchants of the port, when trade was quiet, to turn their hand to piracy. In return, Odd could, and did fall victim to Dutch pirates. English ships could also suffer acts of piracy, with theft and murder committed by raiders from Flanders, Germany and Norway.

In 1282, King Eric of Norway sent a letter to King Edward I regarding Conrad de Stayne, a Prussian merchant from Elvyng. His ship had been cast ashore at Ravenser and all men, except five had drowned. The contents of the ship, wool-fells and a chest of gold and silver coins were stolen by the locals. (RO p24, PRO SC 1 / 19 / 171) It was not until 1296 that a commission was set up to examine the claim, on the understanding that if restitution was made, none of the goods were to pass to France and in no way was Conrad to communicate with the king's enemies. (RO p24, CPR 1292 – 1301 p216)

In 1295 a complaint was received from merchants of Germany and Holland (surely part of the Hanseatic League) concerning three ships bound for Odd laden with herring and other goods. Apparently, they were assaulted by merchants from Lynn, with six of their men killed, and the ships taken to Yarmouth. (RO p23, CPR 1252 – 1301 p215) The boot was on the other foot when the men of Odd complained that the Bishop of Utrecht had not ordered the merchants of Groningen to pay some outstanding debts. (RO p25, CCR 1307 – 1313 p44)

A parliament held early in the reign of Edward II resolved to try and reduce the dual depredations. The Earl of Holland was represented by Christian de Paphurst, and between both parties they would hear and address the many grievances. One such letter, dated 14th January, 1310, was from merchants of Odd, who were applying for a resolution of the matter, on behalf of;

'Peter Attsee and John his son, Walter de Cakhowe, John de Bradele, Thomas de Stamelmere, Richard Trunk, and John Trenthemer, our burgesses and merchants of Ravenesere, who lately, by certain men of your dominions [the Earl of Holland's dominion] were robbed of their goods and merchandise, to the amount of £461 14s 8d., as with grievous complaint they have shown unto us.' (LTH p24, OP p157)

It would appear that the matter was not settled, for the executors of Peter's will were still pursuing the claim in 1320. We find in 1321, a cargo of wool and hides was loaded at Hull on a ship called le Garland, freighted to John Trenchemer of Ravenser Odd. The items belonged to Peter ate See and his son, John, and the count's malefactors captured the cargo, intended for France. The king ordered that goods of the count's subjects were to be seized in various ports in order to recompense the executors mentioned above. There was another, similar case the same year. Richard Trunk and John le Stater had loaded a ship, le Mariole, with wheat, hides, wool and tallow at Hull. This cargo was also bound for France, and once again was seized by the count's malefactors. (RO p26, CCR 1318 – 1323 p396) Throughout the year further cases are recorded. Peter de Wellewyk's ship, laden with wheat, rye and other goods for Denmark, was seized and his son slain. (RO p26, CCR 1318 – 1323 p309) These were indeed lawless times for the traders. In 1315 trading was being disrupted by the lack of clear rules. It was ordered that no-one should be made liable for the debts of associates or because he had acted as guarantor, nor for the criminal acts of others. Traders must also be permitted to sell freely their goods and chattels, provided they paid the customary fees. (RO p27, CPR 1313 – 1317 p273)

At this time there are a number of commissions of 'oyer and terminer' (which literally means 'to hear and determine' in the cases of misdemeanour) regarding cases of assault at Ravenser Odd, and also forestalling of herrings, victuals and other wares destined for local ports. (RO p27, CPR 1313 – 1317 p594) It would appear that many traders, both natives and foreigners were avoiding the port due to extortion there. ((RO p27, CPR 1313 – 1317 p582)

In 1318 there was a commission of oyer and terminer to investigate the complaint of a merchant of Almain about a raid on his ship near Odd. They killed the master and other members of the crew and took the ship and cargo to the port and sold them there. It would appear that the culprits were Stephen atte See and Walter atte Kryke, both of Odd, and some men from Grimsby. (RO p28, CPR 1317 – 1321 p284, p360, p366)

There was further piracy in 1346, when Henry de Brus de Lubyk and others attacked William de Lythnay. (OP p270) It would appear that the merchant was robbed of his goods, to the value of over £186 near

Ravenserod, and his attackers took him to Stralsund and put him in prison. In 1347 or 1348, he sought recourse to parliament for justice. (LTH p40, Rotuli Parliamentorum ii, p207)

However, in the midst of piracy, there was also much honest trade. 1315 was the start of several years of appalling harvests, and the following January, William Payleve (one of the two M.P.s for Ravenser Odd) was granted protection to travel to various parts of the country to purchase corn and other victuals for his family. (RO p28, CPR 1313 – 1317 p380) Another resident, Stephen atte See, who was to be named above as one of the culprits in an act of piracy in 1318, was also given similar protection. (RO p28, CPR 1313 – 1317 p382) In February, it was the turn of John de Cotes to search for food, provided he gave security to the bailiffs where he bought the corn that he would not take it out of the realm. (RO p29, CPR 1313 – 1317 p399) Walter de Cakhou in turn followed the others in his quest for food, giving the same security. (RO p29, CPR 1313 – 1317 p400)

For what could appear an ungodly place, the town did in fact have a house of worship, but not a church, only a chapel built in honour of the Blessed Virgin Mary, which was under the jurisdiction of Easington church. It was most probably built of cobbles from the shore, a common construction material in these parts (parts of Easington church dating from the 13th century, and Skeffling church, which was built in the mid 15th century, make extensive use of this medium). We do not know when the chapel was built, but it was certainly in situ in 1272, when it was in the hands of one Sir Roger Marmyoun, the rector of the church of Easington. The Chronicle of Meaux or Chronica Monasterii de Melsa, between the years 1270 and 1280, tells us:

'In those days a composition was made between the abbot of Albermarl and Sir Roger Marmyoun, rector of the church of Esyngton, in reference to the chapels of Skeftlynge and Ravenserodd, by the intervention of Sir Walter Gyiffard, the archbishop [of York]; so that the chapel of Skeftlynge should remain in the hands of the said abbot, and the chapel of Ravensere Odd should be for ever incorporated with the said church of Esyngton, and that that church of Esyngton should for ever pay to the aforesaid abbot of Albermarl, in lieu of certain tithes, 23 shillings yearly.' (LTH p43, CM ii p153)

In the time when Hugh of Leven was abbot of Meaux (1339 – 1349), he induced John de Cotyngham, the rector of Easington to resign his living, and the abbey eventually appropriated Easington church, and hence the dependant chapels at Ravenser Odd and Skeffling.

As to the materials used in the construction of the rest of the town, cobbles may have been a common and plentiful building resource available locally, but we cannot dismiss the notion that there could have been some brick buildings at this time. Of course, timber and also wattle and daub would have been commonly used, but it is possible that the better structures utilised brick. The famous local family of De la Pole, whose fortunes were made in Odd, had commenced brick and tile making at Trippett, a location near Myton, east of Hull c1303 (VCH Vol 1 p57). Furthermore, bricks were being made near Hedon Haven in the late 14th century (VCH Vol 5 p175). Also, as a seaport, it would have been relatively easy for the town to import Belgian bricks from Bruge if required.

To end this chapter, we look at an interesting document that has survived the passage of the centuries. The will below is of one of the burgesses of the town, and it mentions a number of residents and also gives some insight into the place in the early 14th century. The gentleman must have been a wealthy man, for he had interests in other towns as well as Odd. The quote is a conflation from the three texts noted at the end, as they all differ somewhat.

'Alexander Cocks, of Ravenser-odd, by will there dated, on Wednesday next after the feast of St. James (July 25th), in the year

1327, gives his soul to God almighty, St. Mary, and all the saints, and his body to be buried in the chapel yard (cemetrio capelle). He gives his best animal for his mortuary, and six shillings and eight pence to provide wax to burn about his body on his burial day. To the poor he leaves 30s, and 40s more to be expended on the convening of his friends. To the fabric of St. Mary, at Ravenser-odd, he bequeaths 6s 8d, to William, the chaplain thereof, 2s, to seven other chaplains celebrating in the said chapel, 12d each. To John the clerk serving the said chapel 6d.

To his son and heir, Peter, he devised all his property in Kingston upon Hull, and a plot in Ravenser Odd, with the buildings thereupon, lying between the property of Thomas Coas on one side and that of Geoffrey Champion on the other. To his son, Thomas he gave a plot in Ravenser Odd, with the buildings thereupon, lying between the property of Richard Doncaster on one side, and the common lane on the other. He also gave Thomas annual rents of 15s from the property in which Laurence Lygeard was living, and of 4s 6d. from the property in which Gilbert Prest was living, in Ravenser odd; and a windmill in Hull, given to the testator by Walter De La Grane. To Alexander his son, he left the property in Ravenser Odd in which the testator was living, a plot with buildings opposite, and his messuage lying on the Humber which had been given to him by John son of Hugh Cocks. He also gave to Alexander two shops in 'la Kirke lane', and all his land in Out Newton. To his sister Emma he left an annual payment of 30s from two shops at the bridge foot of Whitby, for her life. To his son Thomas, and his heirs, he gave the reversion of a yearly rent of 4s 6d. The residue of his effects he left to Alice his wife, appointing his sons Peter and Alexander, Stephen de Newton and Sir William Langedik, chaplain, as his executors.'
(ROLEYT p 151 – 152, LTH p55, GP Vol 2 p534)

At the time that this will was written, the port was in its prime, but serious depredations of the sea were soon to follow. Alexander Cocks could not have envisaged that forty years hence, there was to be no town, and certainly no dwelling places to leave to his descendants.

Grimsby complains!

The rise of a new sea port on the opposite bank of the Humber had not gone unnoticed by the rival harbour of Grimsby, and by 1275 the men of that town complained to the king. Hull soon joined their ranks in objecting to a diversion of trade to this upstart. They accused the men of Ravenser of trying to divert ships and their cargoes to Ravenser rather than the other two ports, using fair or foul means. This practice was called 'forestalling'. They further expressed the opinion that the traders of Ravenser spread lies about Grimsby, suggesting that captains would receive poor prices if they berthed there. Obviously, the traders of the Odd strenuously denied these charges. They were just capitalising on the obvious geographical advantage of a port much nearer the sea than Grimsby, and certainly Hull. Here we refer to a contemporary document;

'the island is nearer the sea than the town of Grimsby. And because ships can more easily harbour there than at Grimsby, almost all ships stay, discharge and sell there. Some men (their names are Walter son of Ralph Selby, William Brown, Peter of the Sea and Hugh of Cotes, together with others unknown), go out with their little boats to ships in the Humber and in the sea, that are laden with various goods, and bring the merchants and sailors to harbour in Ravenser.' (ROLEYT, p. 151, Calendar of Inquisitions Miscellaneous i, p211)

The crews of the ships thus forestalled were apparently told by the Ravenser men that the merchants of Grimsby would only pay them 20 shillings for a last of herrings, when in truth they were worth 40 shillings. (RO p11, Calendar of Inquisitions, Miscellaneous, 1219 – 1317, No 1512) That the port of Odd was new can be deduced from the following account;

'Fishermen dried their nets there and men began to live there and afterwards ships began to discharge and sell.' The account then continues that about forty years previously a ship had been wrecked there 'where there was no house, and a man appropriated it, and made a hut, which he inhabited for so long that he received sailors and merchants, and sold food and drink; and afterwards others began to live there, but thirty years past there were not more than four dwelling houses.' (RO p5, Cal. Inquisitions Misc., 1219 – 1317, No 1512)

Furthermore, in another document, the men of Grimsby expanded their grievances by adding the above charge of forestalling, stating that their region was being injured to the amount of £100 a year (a different source says 100 marks, that is, just over £66 per annum [RO p11, Calendar of Inquisitions, Miscellaneous, 1219 – 1317, No 1512]);

'that the men of the said town of Ravenserodd go out with their boats (batelli) into the high sea, where there are ships carrying merchandise, and intending to come to Grimsby with their merchandise. The said men hinder those ships [from coming to Grimsby], and lead them to Ravenser by force when they cannot amicably persuade them to go thither.'
(LTH p 13, Rotuli Hundredorum i, p292)

What further incensed the citizens of Grimsby, and to a lesser extent, Hull, Hedon and Scarborough, was the fact that Ravenser Odd behaved as though it were a borough, (RO p10, Hundred Rolls I, p107, p264) and that tallage, a land or property tax, was not being charged there, creating an unfair advantage. The town, under the oversight of Isabella de Fortibus in the 1260s (she died in 1293 with no heir, and the estate went to the king) certainly operated as though it was already a borough, a privilege not granted until 1299. The town, acting as though a borough, apparently took toll from every ship laden with herrings. (RO p12, Calendar of Inquisitions, Miscellaneous, 1219 – 1317, No 1512)

In their defence, the citizens of Ravenser Odd replied;

'They say that Isabella, countess of Albermarl, by Robert Hildyard her bailiff takes toll at Od; namely, of the nets of all ships brought to land for the purposes of being dried, 4d. And the men of Od distain for their debts as in a borough. And the said countess makes there a port, and causes it to be rebuilt, whereby the king's ports of Grimesby, Scardeburg and Hedon, are greatly injured. And there she holds a court as in a borough. They know not by what warrant.'
(LTHp13, Rotuli Hundredorum i, p107)

The additional complaint about the charging of tallage was most vociferously expounded by Hedon, as recorded in an inquisition of 1280;

'the men of Hedon are straitened and poor; many of them wish to move away on account of being tallaged; they have near them two other good towns, Ravenserodd and Hull, which have good harbours and grow day by day; and if they go there they will dwell without paying tallage.' (NTMA p88, Yorkshire Inquisitions i, p216)

In the matter of the charge of forestalling, things finally came to a head on August 1st 1290, when the king issued a writ that an inquiry was to be held early in September at Grimsby, the substance of which is printed below;

'Edward, by the grace of God king of England, lord of Ireland, and Duke of Aquitaine, to his beloved and faithful Gilbert de Thorneton and Robert de Schaddewrth, saluting. Because we learn from the grave complaint of the mayor and our burgesses of Grymesby that whereas ships with wines, fishes, herrings and other merchandise from various foreign and home parts have been accustomed to harbour in the port of that town and not elsewhere in those parts, and to sell those goods and merchandise there, and to pay the customs thence arising in part payment of the farm of that our town by the hand of our bailiffs there, the bailiffs and men of Isabella de Fortibus, countess of Albemarl, of the town of Ravenserod, which she has caused to be built anew in a certain island within the sea distant ten or twelve leagues (leucae) from the aforesaid town of Grymesby, have arrested for a long time with a strong hand in the sea the ships with the goods contained in them, which in this way have been accustomed so to harbour in our port aforesaid, and with threatening and force have compelled, and from day to day do compel them to turn aside to the aforesaid new town and remain there, and there to sell their merchandise, so that these our men, by such compulsion and subtraction, are so impoverished that they are not able to pay us the debt due to us for the farm of the aforesaid town, unless such ships may be able to harbour at our port aforesaid without hindrance of the said men of Ravenserod, as they were before that town was founded. And they have been accustomed to hold a certain market, which the said countess causes to be proclaimed and held there without warrant. We, being unwilling any longer to sustain such unprepared injury so done to us or our men aforesaid, but desiring to aid our men if they have been so oppressed with injustice, appoint you to inquire, by the oath as well of knights as of other upright and loyal men of the county of Lincoln, by whom the truth of this matter may be better known, concerning the hindrances and forestalling of ships aforesaid, whether these things have been done to our injury or that of our men, or the depression of our town of Grymesby aforesaid, and by whom, or by whose order [these things have been done], and at what time, and by what warrant, the aforesaid market has been proclaimed and held, and to what amount our aforesaid town of Grymesby, by the aforesaid cause, has been deteriorated . . . also the full truth concerning all other circumstances done there, with the contingencies of every kind. And therefore we command you that on a certain day which shall be appointed for this purpose, you shall go to the aforesaid town of Grymesby, and make inquisition there, and the same . . . shall cause to come before you at Grymesby all and such as well as knights and other upright and loyal men . . . by whom the truth of the matter in the premises may be better known and enquired. In testimony of which these letters . . . we have made patents. Witnessed by me at Leghton, the first day of August in the 18th year of our reign.' (LTH p 14 – 15, Chancery Inquisition, 18 Ed I, No 145)

It did not take long for the king's commissioners to complete their enquiry and report back;

'Inquisition taken at Grumsby on the Sabbath day next after the Nativity of the Blessed Virgin Mary (8th September) in the 18th year of the reign of King Edward, before Gilbert de Thornton and Robert de Schadwrd, appointed by the king's writ to inquire concerning the hindrances and forestallings of ships, which have been laden with various merchandise, and which have been accustomed to come and harbour at Grumsby, done by the men of Rawenserod, and concerning other grievances and injuries to the men of Grumsby by the men of Rawenserod, by which the aforesaid town of Grumsby has been much deteriorated; by the jurors undernamed, namely, Robert de Rochewell, Sayer Scawin, John de Hanley, Robert de Thoresby, Robert de Abingdon, Richard de Newhous, Robert Maundewile, William de St. Paul de Leysebey, Ralph Malet de Irby, Hugh de Brakenberg, John son of Roger de Stalingberg, and Benedict de Leysebey, priest, who say on their oath that in the time of King Henry, father of the present king, at first by the casting up of the sea, a certain small island was born, which is called Rawenserod, which is distant from the town of Grumsby by the space of one tide. And at first fishermen dried their nets there, and a few men begun to dwell and remain there, and afterwards ships laden with various merchandise begun to discharge and sell their merchandise there. And more than this, that the aforesaid island is nearer the sea than the town of Grumsby. And because ships can more easily harbour there than at Grumsby, almost all ships stay, discharge and sell there. They say also that Walter son of Ralph de Seleby, William Brune, Peter de Mari and Hugh de Cotes, together with certain other unknown persons of the island of Rawenserod, according to their custom, go out with their little boats to ships in the Humber and in the sea laden with various

merchandise, and conduct the merchants and sailors to harbour at
Rawenser, saying that the burgesses of Grumsby, after accustomed
manner, cheapen the price of things sold there. And they [i.e., the men
of Ravenserod] say that a last of herrings is worth but twenty shillings
at Grumsby, where [in reality] it is worth forty shillings. So that by
words, offers and bids they detain them so long a time that they cannot
come to the chosen port of Grumsby, so that by such forestalling the
town of Grumsby, in every year after the coronation of the present king
has been impoverished to the amount of 100 marks. They say,
moreover, that the men of the aforesaid town of Grumsby are not able
to pay their farm rent unless [ships] passing Rawenser may harbour at
Grumsby without hindrance at Rawenser:- so that the aforesaid town is
partly abandoned. Asked during what period had men lived at
Ravenserod, they say that forty years ago a certain ship was cast away
on Rawenserod, where there was no house then built, which ship a
certain person appropriated to himself, and from it made for himself a
cabin (scala sive casa) which he inhabited for some time, that there he
received ships and merchants and sold them meat and drink, and
afterwards others begun to dwell there; and they say that about 30 years
ago there were no more than four houses (mansiones) there. They say
also that before the last four years the men of Grumsby who bought
herrings and other merchandise from fishermen and others coming with
their ships to Grumsby, did not at once pay the price, but reckoned
wrongly with the aforesaid merchants, and cheapened that price, and
made the merchants stay there until they were satisfied; and this is
another reason why ships do not harbour at Grumsby, as they were
accustomed to do. And on account of this fact the town is deteriorated
to the amount of 40 pounds. But they say truly that now they faithfully
pay those merchants the price agreed between them, and cheapen
nothing thereof, so that all merchants coming thither with their
merchandise are satisfied within three tides. And they say that Isabella
de Fortibus, countess of Albermarl, is lady of the aforesaid island, and
takes the profits thereof. and that the men dwelling there, every day, at
their own free will, buy and sell fish and herrings and other victuals and

other merchandise, nor is there any fixed day to hold a market there. They say, moreover, that the men of Rawenserod take toll, after the manner of a borough, of ships and other merchandise coming thither, as well as those of Grumsby as of other places, namely, of every ship with a rudder laden with herrings, for each last of herrings contained in a ship, 4d., and of every boat (batellus) for each last of herrings, 1d. And of other ships and boats laden with any other kind of merchandise . . . toll . . . they know not how much. In witness whereof the jurors of this inquisition have affixed their seal.' (LTH p15 – 16, Chancery Inquisition, 18 Edward I, No 145)

This result did not please the men of Grimsby, for they lost on a technicality; the narration only extended to forestalling and impoverishment of Grimsby and not to trespass done against the king's peace. To make matters worse for them, they were amerced for making a false claim! (RO p12, PRO Coram Rege Roll, Mich. 19 Edw I KB 27 / 129) However, it appears that the men of this town were not blameless in these matters. Apparently, in times past they had been guilty of 'mis-pricing' goods brought into the port. Incidentally, the measure a 'last' of herrings, was a unit of quantity varying between 13,200 fish by Saxon measurement, and 10,000 fish as decided by Parliament in 1644. The following is a translation of the record of the case;

'Walter, son of Ralph de Seleby, William Brun, Peter de la mer, Hugh de Paul, Roger Fhys, Derman son of Walter, Priest John de Drax, John de Bradele, William Whyt, John Acard, William de Araz, Henry del Ward, Richard Gril, Richard le Serjeant, Hugh Keling, Walter de Cathone, Peter le Whyte, Hugh Eren, Simon Atte Se, Walter Pyngel, Richard Shail, Robert de Cotes, Richard le Taverner steward of Beverley, Thomas Chusur, John de Crull, Alan de Skardeburgh, Gilbert Trewe, Alexander Cok, Hugh Knote, Stephen de Patrington, Thomas Chaumpeneys, Roger le Bucher, , William de Hill, William Rose, John Rose and Walter Atte Chirche were attached to respond to the pleading of the mayor and commonality of Grymesby, for what reasons they had violently arrested, by various forces, various merchants, as well foreign as native, both in the sea and in the water of the Humber, with their ships and boats laden with wines, fish and various other merchandise, directing their course towards the aforesaid town of Grymesby, and wishing to harbour in that port, in order to deal there with the merchandise aforesaid, and had compelled them to go to the town of Ravensrod and there to harbour, to remain and to sell their aforesaid merchandise, and in this way have forestalled against the usage at this day practised in the king's dominion, and to the same extent by the mayor and commonality aforesaid. And other irregular things, etc., to the no little injury of that mayor and commonality, and their manifest impoverishment, and against the peace, etc. and it was inquired whence it was that when certain merchants, with their ships and boats laden with the merchandise aforesaid, namely Lambert Wolf, William son of John de Flyeneye, and John son of Brun, and various other merchants, directing their course towards the said town of Grymesby, and wishing to harbour there, to deal with the merchandise aforesaid, the aforesaid Walter and others, on the Monday next before the feast of the Nativity of the Blessed Mary [8th September], in the first year of the reign of our present king [1273], arrested the aforesaid Lambert and others and compelled them to go to the town of Ravensrod, and to harbour and sell their merchandise there, and in this way have forestalled against the usage of the king's dominion, at this day observed by the same mayor and commonality, whence they say that they have been deteriorated and have had injury done them to the amount of five thousand pounds, and herein they produce their suit, etc.

And the aforesaid Walter and others, by Robert de Cave their attorney come to defend, etc. And they say they ought not to respond to this writ, because they say that in the aforesaid writ, or in the narration of the aforesaid commonality, there is not contained any fact which is done to the aforesaid commonality of Grymesby against the peace of the king, not even by the forestalling of the aforesaid commonality, and the impoverishment of the aforesaid town of Grymesby; whence they pray judgement on the aforesaid writ, etc.

And the aforesaid mayor and commonality of Grymesby, by William de Hauden their attorney, say that the aforesaid writ, and also their narration, testify sufficiently to the transgression against the peace of the king done to them, whence they pray judgment, etc. And because it is stated in the writ that something in this way had been done against the peace of the king, and in the narration it is not stated that any injury was done to the aforesaid commonality of Grymesby, except in this that they of Ravensere had forestalled the men of Grymesby by buying merchandise from merchants willing to harbour at the port of Grymesby, and in this way the narration extends only to forestalling and the impoverishment of the town of Grymesby, and not to a trespass done to the aforesaid commonality of Grymesby against the king's peace, it is apparent that the aforesaid mayor and commonality of Grymesby gain nothing by their writ, but are at the king's mercy for a false claim. And the aforesaid Walter son of Ralph and others therein…..' (LTH p17 – 18, Coram Rege Roll, Michaelmas term, 19 Ed I, No 130)

Having been exonerated of the charges laid at their door, the merchants of Ravenser Odd proceeded to capitalise on the undoubted advantages that the port possessed.

Ravenser becomes a borough

Through the influence of the Count of Aumale, the town behaved as though it was a borough from as early as 1250. However, it did not gain this status officially until 1299, a few months after the king had visited East Yorkshire. The king was often in the north, travelling to deal with the claimants to the Scottish throne. Indeed, to all intents and purposes the centre of government between 1298 and 1304 was York, when the Court of the King's Bench and the Exchequer were there, and Edward I often visited Burstwick.

The presentation made by Ravenser Odd to the king at Cottingham at Christmas 1298, when he was a guest of Lord John de Wake, was that they desired to be a free borough, and offered to pay the sum of £300 (450 marks) to achieve this end. Hull, which applied at the same time only had to pay 100 marks, that is £66, to become the borough of Kingston upon Hull. This could suggest the king's favour towards Hull. In the mercantile free trade nature of Ravenser, the town was tardy in paying this fine for their charter of liberties. In the year 1299 – 1300, the burgers had only paid £36, and it was to be another three years before the balance of £264 was finally paid. (LTH p22, Frost's Notices p57)

The men of Ravenser Odd had a number of requests, in particular; that they might have a coroner (who could deal with wrecks); a warden to be appointed by the king, and their own prison and gallows. They also asked for a fair, to be held each year from Candlemas for thirty days, and two markets per week on a Tuesday and Saturday (They were granted the Tuesday, but then given Sunday rather than Saturday). (ROLEYT p151)

It may be noted that the original market day, chosen in 1250 when the town has assumed the status of borough, was Thursday. Both the Ravenser and the Hull petitions were referred to the Lord Treasurer and the Barons of the Exchequer. After due consideration and investigation, both were granted, in the case of Odd, on the 1st of April 1299. Boyle contains a translation of this charter, which I have reproduced below.

'Edward, by the grace of God king of England, lord of Ireland and duke of Aquitaine, to the archbishops, bishops, abbots, priors, earls, barons, justices, sheriffs, provosts, ministers, and to all his bailiffs and faithful subjects, greeting. Be it known that, for the improvement of our said town of Ravenserode, and for the utility and profit of our men of that town, we will grant for us and our heirs, that our town aforesaid from henceforth shall be a free borough, and the men of the same town shall be free burgesses, and shall have for ever all the liberties and free customs belonging to a free borough. So that nevertheless that borough shall be kept by some faithful man, to be appointed thereto successively by us and our heirs, who shall first take corporal oath to the burgesses aforesaid, in the holy gospels of God, that he will preserve unhurt all the liberties granted by us to the same burgesses and borough, and faithfully and diligently do all those things which pertain to the office of warden in the borough aforesaid. We have granted also for us and our heirs, that the aforesaid burgesses and their heirs and successors may devise lands and tenements, which they have within the same borough, or which they may have hereafter, by their last will, freely and without hindrance of us, or our heirs or our bailiffs whomsoever, to whomsoever they will. And that they shall have the return of all our writs in any manner relating to that borough. So that no sheriff or other bailiff or minister of ours shall enter that borough, to execute any office there for anything belonging to that borough, except in default of the same warden. And they shall not implead or be impleaded elsewhere than within the same borough, before the aforesaid warden, concerning any tenures within that manor, or trespasses or contracts made within the same borough, before the aforesaid warden, concerning any tenures within that manor, or trespasses or contracts made within the same borough And also that those burgesses and their heirs by writs of our chancery shall choose a coroner from among themselves, and present him to the said warden, before whom he shall make oath that he will faithfully do and preserve those things which pertain to the office of coroner in the said borough. And moreover he will grant for us and our heirs, that a certain prison shall be made and had in the same borough for the punishment of malefactors there apprehended, and that gallows likewise shall be erected outside the borough aforesaid on our own proper soil so that the aforesaid warden may execute judgement concerning infangthef and outfangthef.

Moreover we will and grant for us and our heirs, that the said burgesses and their heirs shall for ever quit, throughout all our kingdom and dominion, of toll, pontage, passage, pavage, and murage and of all other customs payable for their own goods and merchandise. And that all those of the borough aforesaid desiring to enjoy the liberties and free customs aforesaid shall be taxed at geld and scot with the same burgesses, whenever it shall happen to that borough (to be taxed). Moreover we grant, for us and our heirs, to the aforesaid burgesses, that they and their heirs shall have for ever two markets in every week within the borough aforesaid, to be held in a place appointed by us for that purpose, that is to say, one on Tuesday and the other on the Sunday, and one fair there in each year to continue for thirty days, that is to say, on the vigil, on the day and on the morrow of the Nativity of the blessed Mary, and for twenty-seven days next following; unless those markets, and that fair shall be to the injury of neighbouring markets and fairs. Wherefore we will and firmly command for us and our heirs that the aforesaid town shall from henceforth be a free borough, and the men of the same town shall be free burgesses, and shall have all the liberties and free customs belonging to a free borough forever. So that nevertheless that borough shall be kept by some faithful man, successively chosen for that purpose by us and our heirs, who first shall take corporal oath to the burgesses aforesaid, on the holy gospels of God that he will preserve unhurt all the liberties granted by us to the same burgesses and borough, and shall faithfully and diligently do all those things which pertain to the office of warden in the borough aforesaid. And that the aforesaid burgesses and their heirs and successors may devise their lands and tenements which they have within the same borough, and which they shall have hereafter, in their last will, to whomsoever they will, freely and without hindrance of us or our heirs or bailiffs whomsoever. And that they shall have the return of all our writs in any manner relating to that borough. So that no sheriff or other bailiff or minister of ours shall enter that borough, to execute any office there, for anything pertaining to that borough, except in default of the same warden. And that they shall not implead or be impleaded elsewhere than within the same borough, before the warden aforesaid, concerning any tenures within that manor, or trespasses or contracts made within the same borough. And also that the same burgesses and their heirs, by writs of our chancery, shall choose a coroner from among themselves, and shall present him to the said warden, before whom he shall make oath that he will faithfully do and preserve those things which pertain to the office of coroner in the said borough. And that a certain prison shall be made and had in the same borough, for the punishment of malefactors there apprehended, and gallows likewise erected outside the borough aforesaid on our own proper soil. So that the aforesaid warden may execute judgment of infangthef and outgangthef. And that the aforesaid burgesses and their heirs shall be for ever quit, throughout all our kingdom and dominion, of toll, pontage, passage, pavage and murage, and all other customs payable for their own proper goods and merchandise. And that all those of the borough aforesaid, desirous to enjoy the liberties and free customs aforesaid, shall be taxed at geld and scot with the same burgesses, whenever it shall happen to that borough [to be taxed]. And that the same burgesses and their heirs shall have forever the aforesaid markets and fair within the borough aforesaid, with all liberties and free customs pertaining to these markets and fair; except those markets and fair shall be to the injury of neighbouring markets and fairs, as is aforesaid. These are witnesses: The venerable father W. bishop of Coventry and Lichfield, Henry de Lacy earl of Lincoln, Henry de Percy, John Tregoz, Walter de Bello Campo steward of our household, Roger Brabazon,

John de Metingham, Peter Mallore, Walter de Gloucester and others,
Given by our hand at Westminster, the first day of April, in the twenty-
seventh year of our reign [1299].'
(Charter of Inspeximus, Charter Roll, 5 Ed. II., m. 8; as contained in
LTH p20 – 22)

Incidentally, another source records the market days as being Tuesday
and Saturday, not Sunday (RO p13, CCR ii, p476). It may be helpful at
this juncture to explain a few of the terms used in the document.
Infangthef is the right to arrest and try someone within the area of your
jurisdiction, and outfangthef is the right to pursue and arrest them
outside this area. Pontage was a toll for the building or repair of
bridges, and passage was a toll for the right to pass through a certain
place. Pavage was a toll for the maintaining or improvement of roads
and streets, and murage was a toll raised for the building or repair of
town walls. In the case of Ravenser, it is interpreted as required to
provide defences against the sea.

So by 1300, Ravenser Odd had the status of a free borough with
freedom throughout the kingdom from paying tolls, the right to dispose
of land at will, the right to hold a court in town where most non-criminal
disputes could be tried and to be freed from the sheriff's jurisdiction;
to have the king's prison in borough and the gallows without on the
king's soil. (RO p13, CCR ii, p476, VCH Vol 5 p72, CCR 1296 – 1302
p509) It was an important and expanding trading port. There was a
confirmation of the charter by Edward II in 1312, when the men of the
town paid a fine of £50 for quayage for seven years. (LTH p37) A
further fine was paid in 1333 / 34 to procure a confirmation of the
charter. (LTH p38)

On the face of it, with a royal charter, the town was prospering, but by
this time Odd was in serious decline. The burghers of the town could
negotiate with kings and the lords, and manage international trade as
experienced businessmen. Unfortunately, they could not negotiate with

the very medium that made the site prosperous in the first place – the sea. The initial record of money to repair the waterfront had come in the form of a grant of quayage in 1296. It was to be followed by nine more grants over the next fifty years, as Odd gradually lost its battle with the merciless waters. (LTH p18)

Ravenser in the wars

The period covered by the town's existence was a troubled one, for England was often at war with either France or Scotland, or both. Ravenser Odd was seen as a strategic northern port in the event of conflict, especially between 1298 and 1304, when York practically became the capital. (RO p12, VCH Yorkshire Vol 1 p16) In April 1297, Edward I, through an Admiral of the Sea, ordered that all ships of the port of 40 tuns of wine or more be at Winchelsea by midsummer, for an expedition to Flanders. (RO p30, CCR 1296 – 1302 p101, p121). A further demand for a ship, men and necessities was made in 1301, this time to proceed to Berwick on Tweed. Hull, Hedon and Grimsby provided one ship each, and Scarborough two. (RO p30, CCR 1296 – 1302 p483). In 1304, John Bally, master of the Maryole delivered corn to the Prince of Wales at Perth. Roger Maletek, Richard Trunck and Richard de Doncastre were also involved in the corn and salt trade to the Prince and the king in Scotland. (RO p32, PRO E 101 / 11 / 30) With the temporary conquest of Scotland in 1304 things went quiet for a short while.

However, trouble soon flared up again, and from 1310 to 1339 there are numerous mentions of Ravenser's part in the wars with Scotland. At that time, there was no Royal Navy fleet, and so the sovereign of the day would requisition ships, men and victuals as required. In the summer of 1310, Edward II required one war-ship, well equipped with sufficient and defensible men, well furnished with all necessary things, for the start of his campaign. Initially, the king's ships were to sail to Dublin, but this was subsequently altered to proceeding directly to Scotland.

The next request was made on March 12th 1314, for merchants who wished to sell their victuals or armour, to bring them to the parts of Scotland where the king's army might be. The bailiffs also had to take security from the merchants that they would only deliver to the army and not anyone else. On May 9th, the bailiffs commanded that there be no trade with Flanders or elsewhere, only the king's army. Edward was defeated at Bannockburn on July 25th, and he immediately issued mandates for Ravenser, along with many other ports, to supply one ship, men and victuals. The years 1315 to 1317 were famine years, for there was heavy rain, little summer and poor crops. With this in mind, Edward issued a demand in January 1315 that no one should supply Scotland with food, under the severest penalties. To prosecute his next assault on Scotland, the king issued a writ on August 12th for merchants to supply his troops, and no one else, as soon as possible.

Already, we see a pattern emerging; the demand for a suitable ship and men, victuals for said ship, and requests for traders to supply the troops, and not the enemy. This was to be way of things for nearly three decades. I believe that it would be tedious for me to record each call upon the men and merchants of the port, and so I have condensed them into the following list, interspersed with passages from documents of the time.

1319 November 6th. There was a request from the king for certain men to arm themselves before the coming Christmas. The following missive was sent to Alexander Cok and John atte See of Ravenserod;

'Everyone [in the liberty], between the ages of twenty and sixty, having forty shillings worth of land, or chattels of the value of sixty shillings, should have, under the penalties mentioned below, an acketon, a bascinet, and gloves of plate, or more, sufficient for defence, for one man on foot.
And everyone having a hundred shillings worth of land, or chattels to the value of ten marks, should have a horse, an acketon, a hauberk, a bascinet and gloves of plate for a hobbler.
And everyone having ten pounds worth of land, or chattels to the value of twenty pounds, should have equipments and armour as a man of arms.' (LTH p26, Rotuli Scotiae i, p204)

1321 In the spring, a Scottish ship, forced into Ravenser by the weather, was seized. However, as there was a truce on, this action was unlawful. The bailiff was instructed;

'We admonish you that Ivo de Hadyngton and other Scotch men, recently passing along the coast of the sea in a certain ship, with their goods and merchandise, and driven upon the land at Ravenserodd by the fury of the same sea, and arrested by you, together with their goods and merchandise, found in the aforesaid ship,
If it shall appear to you that the said Ivo and the other men, with the goods and merchandise aforesaid, are of Scotland, and have been driven to the said place by the fury of the sea, as has been said, you will cause them to be liberated and disarrested without delay, according to the tenor of the truce aforesaid.' (LTH p26 - 27, Rymer's Foedera iii, p879)

The same year, some people of the town were absolved from previous dealings with Scots. The truce can't have lasted long, for later that year, the king once more required a ship and men. Additionally, he demanded men for his army. The town thought this too much, and sent a petition to Edward;

'To our lord the king and his council, his burgesses of the towns of Ravenserodd and Grimmesbi, which are ports of the sea, pray that, as they are charged by the command of our lord the king to find two ships and two barges, with double equipment, at their own cost, for 40 days, the which are ready furnished to go on the sea, that he will please of his grace to grant to the said burgesses, that they may be discharged from going by land, on account of the great peril which would come to the said towns because of the enemies of the king who are on the sea.'
(LTH p28, Rotuli Parliamentorum i, 405)

In the event, no men were sent for the army.

1322 July 24th. The king thanked the burgesses of Ravenser Odd for their grant of a ship and 30 armed men and victuals, it was to sail to Tynemouth.

1324 May 10th. There were more demands for ships 'carrying 40 tuns of wine or more' for the king's service. This included those in port, and those due in, and the king was to be notified of the likely number. There were warnings of the danger of falling into the hands of adversaries and pirates. (RO p31, CCR 1323 – 1327 p183)

1326 brought a writ from the king to search and arrest suspected persons.

1326 August. Robert de Siwardeby appointed in Odd to ensure that masters and ships join John de Sturmy, Admiral of the fleet in the North. All ships of 30 tons or more to proceed to Orwell in Suffolk by September 21st, with men, victuals and necessities. (RO p32, CCR 1323 – 1327 p643)

1327 May 6th. A mandate was received by the port to supply two ships 'carrying a burden of 60 tons or more, and men and victuals. This demonstrates how important Ravenser was, for only one ship each was required of Grmysby, Wayneflet, Scardeburgh and Whiteby.

In 1332, Edward Baliol departed from Ravenser, and assisted by lords Beaumont, Wake, Mowbray and others, he routed a body of Scots who opposed him and was crowned at Scone.

During the 1330s, we know the names of several ships of the port that were licensed to undertake the king's business; Faucon, whose master was Richard le Ledebeter, and the Rose and Elyne; these two were to bring back wine from Gascony, together with herring and other goods. (RO p32, CPR 1334 – 1338 p111, p338, p339)

1333 April 11th. Once more, the town had an order to supply a ship for an expedition to Scotland. It is repeated here, as it mentions a boat of the port, and its owner;

'The king to the bailiffs and true men of the town of Ravenserodd, greeting. Whereas lately we commanded you that you should cause a ship of war in the port of the town aforesaid of the greater and stronger ships of the same town to be provided and prepared, and that ship to be furnished as well with capable strong men and well and sufficiently armed, as with other necessaries, which might be required; so that the ship so furnished with men and other necessaries, should be ready and prepared on Wednesday in Easter Week last part at the latest, then to depart thence at our charges to the parts of Scotland for our expedition of war thither. And you afterwards, in consideration of an abatement which we made to you one hobbler and six archers to which you had been accessed by the commissioners appointed by us for the array of men in the East Riding of the county of York, granted to us one ship of war, namely, the better [ship] of the same town, for the setting out of our expedition aforesaid, and we commanded William de Ferby of Ravenserodd that he should cause for the reason aforesaid, to come to the said port of Ravenserodd his ship called the Saynte Marie, a cogge of Ravenserodd which is reputed to be the better ship of the said town, and the same William now coming to us, has declared that his said ship was previously sent to foreign parts, and concerning its return he was altogether ignorant. We, therefore, strictly command and enjoin you that you cause the better ship of the town aforesaid, to be provided and prepared for war, and furnished with sailors and other capable and strong men, and well and sufficiently armed, and with other necessities, and to set out with all speed which can be made in our expedition aforesaid, at our charge, towards the parts of Scotland aforesaid. And this ye shall in no wise omit as ye regard us and our honour, and wish to save yourselves harmless. Witnessed by the king at Durham, 11thday of April [1333]. By the king himself.' (LTH p29 – 30, Rotuli Scotiae p228)

It would appear that William de Ferby also owned another ship, the Margarete at Ravenser Odd. (RO p33, CCR 1333 – 1337 p99)

1333 June 16th. Yet another writ, for the bailiff to detain all ships capable of carrying 50 tuns of wine or more, including those due into the port, ready for the king's service. This order was subsequently relaxed on August 16th.

1334. Richard le Taverner and William de Braddele were given protection to take goods to Newcastle and Berwick for the king and his army. (RO p33, CPR 1334 -1338 p38)

1334 September 20th. A writ to several towns, one of which was Ravenser, to supply a ship to arrest ships of the king's enemies, along with their goods, wherever they may be found, and to conduct certain ships of the king's loyal and faithful subjects to their destinations.

1334 December 24th. Once more, a ship of 50 tuns of wine or more, and men was required. This order could lead to mistakes, with foreign ships sometimes being seized. On January 12th 1335 there is record of a command to disarrest these ships, and permit them without hindrance to proceed wherever they wished.

1335 February 1st. Yet another ship was to be requisitioned, and sent to Newcastle on Tyne. On February 22nd, the king relaxed his demands somewhat from other ports, but Ravenser still had to detain one ship for the king's service.

1335 March 6th. Three ships were to be selected from Hull, Ravenser and other ports. John de Hyldesle and William de la Pole were empowered to execute this order.

1336 October 3rd. France had adopted the cause of Scotland, and so there was concern over possible invasion. To this end, royal writs were issued to all ports, including Ravenser to have men and arms ready.

1336 October 5th. A royal writ is issued to the bailiffs of Ravenserod to apprehend all men of Flanders and their ships, merchandise, goods and chattels.

1336 November 6th. With fears of invasion running high, the king commanded that all ships should be made ready to form a convoy at the port of Orwell by December 1st, and to proceed to Spain for wine and other merchandise.

1336 December 13th. The bailiffs of Ravenser were to appoint three or four 'discreet and true men' to attend a council at Norwich, to consult on 'affairs of the nation'.

1337 January 10th. William de Ros and James de Kyngeston were to select ships for service in Scotland, with men sufficiently armed and victuals to last thirteen weeks. Sometime during 1337 or 1338, a certain ship, which was carrying goods for the Scots, was seized at Ravenser, and certain individuals made off with the goods. The king was displeased, and an enquiry was made as to their whereabouts.

1338 July 28th. Vessels often required safe passage to Scotland, and this was the case of the 'Radegund' of Ravenser. The document is of interest, not only for the ships' name, but also its locally esteemed owner, Robert Rotenheryng;

'The king to all and singular, the admirals, bailiffs, ministers, and all other his faithful subjects, as well within his liberties as without, to whom, etc., greeting.
Know ye that whereas our beloved Robert Rotenheryng proposes to load a certain ship, called the 'Radegunde' of Ravensere, with various

kinds of corn and other victuals in the port of Ravensere, and to carry them to the parts of Scotland, as far as the town of St. John of Perth, and our castles of Coupre in Fyf, Stryvelyn and Edenburgh, to sell them there for the sustenance of our faithful subjects occupied in the defence of the town and castles aforesaid; we have taken under our protection and defence the same Robert, and his men and servants, and the mariners of the ship aforesaid, in going with the ship with the grain and victuals aforesaid, to the parts aforesaid, remaining there, and returning thence. And therefore we command you, that you do not inflict, or so far as in you lies, permit to be inflicted by others, any injury, molestation, damage, hindrance or any other grievance upon the same Robert, or his men and servants or the mariners aforesaid, in going with the ship, corn, and victuals aforesaid, to the parts aforesaid, remaining there, and returning thence, as is aforesaid, etc, etc.' (LTH p35, Rotuli Scotiae i, p539)

1339 June 2nd. Another grant of safe passage was given to Hull and Ravenser ships. Again it names vessels and their masters, and so is included here;

'The king to all and singular the sheriffs, mayors, bailiffs, ministers and other faithful subjects, as well within his liberties as without, to whom, etc., greetings. Know ye that whereas our beloved and faithful Thomas de Rokeby, keeper of our castles of Stryvelyn and Edeneburgh in Scotland, has freighted at Kyngeston upon Hull and Ravensere three ships called the Eleyne of Ravensere, the Laurence of Hull, and the Michel of Hull, of which John Kelyng, Richard de Birkyng, and John le Vanne are masters, to carry victuals and other things for the sustenance of the said Thomas, etc, etc' (LTH p36, Rotuli Scotiae i, p568)

1346. Despite the increasing destruction by the sea, the port was still expected to supply one ship and 28 mariners for the king to lay siege to Cressy in that year! However, to put this in context, Hull sent 16 ships and 466 mariners, and Grimsby 11 vessels and 171 mariners. (RO p38, LTH p38)

This concludes Ravenser's part in the conflicts with Scotland and France. Unless stated otherwise, all the information noted above came from records in the rolls entitled 'Rotuli Scotiae', and reproduced in Boyle's 'Lost Towns of the Humber'.

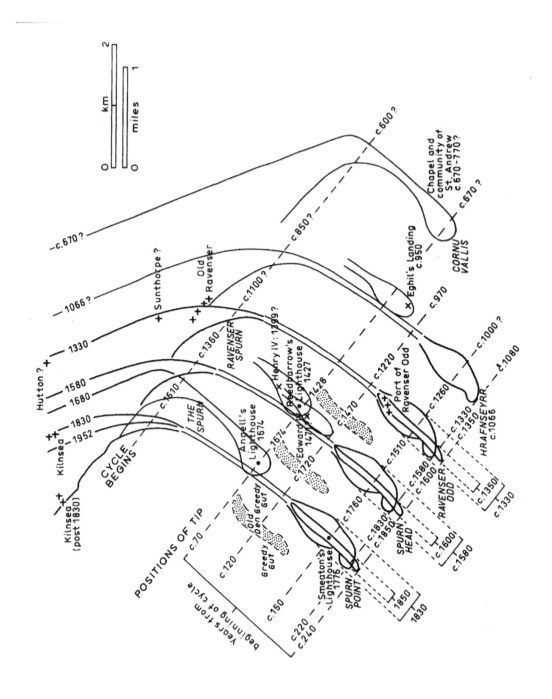

Diagram of the Spurn cyclical theory as propounded by George De Boer in 1964.
Courtesy of the De Boer estate.

The People

Ultimately, the history of any town is a cumulative chronicle of the lives of the folk who were born, lived and died there. The houses, wharves, halls, sheds and churches are physical evidence of their endeavours and labours in transforming an uninhabited location into a thriving and prosperous community. Their existence lives on in the physicality of their established domain – it is the crystallised embodiment of all their labours.

The same was true of Ravenser until the waters consigned their essence to a watery oblivion. However, their memory lingers on in the documents that have survived the intervening centuries. Their names appear as echoes of a former age on parchments of legal and ecclesiastical import.

This wealth of information about these individuals has appeared in all previous books about Ravenser. However, their names usually appear within the body of the text, as part of the narrative flow of the chapter, and there has never been any attempt to draw up a comprehensive catalogue of all their names. Therefore, I have decided to adopt an entirely different approach, and list them alphabetically in this chapter, along with any activity with which they are connected, and noting the reference from the various court rolls etc and books that have made note of these long lost characters. If there is no entry after their name, then their name lives on, but their story, and the part they played in the town of Ravenser, has been lost.

First, a note about nomenclature. Spelling of surnames often varies from document to document, and over the years. For the sake of completeness, I have tried to make logical assumptions on the spelling of family names. Also, it is fairly evident that, say, Peter Att See, could be interpreted, in the light of Norman influence, to be also called Peter De La Mare. If this has occurred, I have listed both entries, and directed the reader between the two. Additionally, if a name spans an unnatural period, one has to assume that more than one person bore that name.

One should not assume that every person listed below resided in Ravenser, only that they are recorded as having links with the town, usually commercial. With some difficulty, I have attempted to exclude persons named as sitting on various councils and inquisitions at different times. Often they are independent witnesses to the legal process, called from neighbouring areas. The texts are often obscure in their usage of English, and have to be read carefully to extract the roles played by each person named.

Acard, John, mentioned at the end of the forestalling inquisition 1291 (LTH p17)
Atte Chirche, Walter, Rose, John, mentioned at the end of the forestalling inquisition 1291 (LTH p17)
Atte Kyrke, Walter, involved in an act of piracy, killing a master and bringing the ship to Ravenser Odd 1318 (RO p28)
Atte See, Alice, wife of the first John, died 1345 (LTH p52) also De Mari?
Atte Se, Emma, wife of Peter (LTH p52) also De Mari?
Atte See, Hugh, to appear on behalf of Ravenser at a council at Westminster 1337 (OP p141) also De Mari?
Att See, John, (there were two of them) burgess and merchant remonstrating to parliament about piracy by Holland 1310 (OP p155) complaint about piracy 1310 (LTH p24) commissioned to raise men to fight against the Scots 1323 (OP p160) died 1349 (LTH p52) John, son of John, owned a vacant place at Ravensrod called Locksmith Lane 1336 (OP p270) manucaptor for Peter ate See as M.P. for Ravenser 1304 (LTH p23) John, son of John, M.P. for Ravenser 1327 (LTH p23) raising men for the king's army 1319 (LTH p26) mentioned in a scutage roll of 1359 (LTH p52) also De Mari?
Atte See, Margaret, wife of the second John (LTH p52)

Atte See, Peter, defendant in the suit of the burgesses of Grimsby 1291 (LTH p52) one of the first members of parliament from Ravenser Odd 1304 (OP p141) burgess and merchant remonstrating to parliament about piracy by Holland 1310 (OP p155) had a grant of the manor of Tharlesthorp c1315 (LTH p52) died in 1318 - 19, petition regarding his will mentioned in the reigns of Edward II and III (LTH p51) also De Mari?

Atte Se, Simon, mentioned at the end of the forestalling inquisition 1291 (LTH p17) also De Mari?

Atte See, Stephen, involved in an act of piracy, killing a master and bringing the ship to Ravenser Odd 1318 (RO p28) also De Mari?

Balli, William, manucaptor for William Pailleleve as M.P. for Ravenser 1304 (LTH p23)

Bally, John, master of the ship called Maryole, delivered corn to the household of the Prince of Wales 1304 (RO p32)

Barell, Alan, carucate of land in Ald Ravense, date not given (OP p181)

De Barton, John, the king granted dues and customs of the ports of Kingston upon Hull and Ravensrod to him 1326 (OP p160)

Brune, William, merchant of Ravenser accused of forestalling 1290 (LTH p15) merchant mentioned at the end of the inquisition 1291 (LTH p17)

Campion, (Champion) Geoffrey or Galfrid, manucaptor for Thomas le Taverner as M.P. for Ravenser 1326 (LTH p23) mentioned in Alexander Cock's will as having a tenement at Ravenser next to his 1327 (ROLEYT p152)

Chese, John, present at the baptism of John ate See 1311 (RO p21)

Chaumpeneys, Thomas, mentioned at the end of the forestalling inquisition 1291 (LTH p17)

Chusur, Thomas, mentioned at the end of the forestalling inquisition 1291 (LTH p17)

Coas, Thomas, mentioned in Alexander Cock's will as having a tenement at Ravenser next to his 1327 (LTH p55)

Cock Alisaundre, commissioned to raise men to fight against the Scots 1323 (OP p160) see below Cok or Coke

Cocks, Alice, wife of Alexander, mentioned in his will (LTH p55)
Cocks, John, son of Hugh Cocks, mentioned in the will of Alexander
Cocks (LTH p55)
Cocks, Peter, son of Alexander, executor of his will (LTH p55)
Cok, (Coke) Alexander, mentioned at the end of the forestalling
inquisition 1291 (LTH p17) raising men for the king's army 1319 (LTH
p26) will of Alexander Cocks of Ravenser-odd 1327 (LTH p55) also
had a son called Alexander, mentioned in his father's will as to inherit
his tenement in Ravenser-odd 1327, also executor of his will (LTH p55)
same as Cock above?
Coke, Peter, son of Alexander, to be left property in Ravenser in his
father's will 1327 (LTH p55) died 1352 (RO p18), but one messuage
with its appurtenances was still held in his name in Ravenser 1359 - 60
(LTH p56)
Coke, Thomas, son of Alexander, mentioned in Alexander Cock's will
to inherit a place, with buildings thereon 1327 (LTH p55)
Danthorp, Matthew, a hermit at Ravenspurne, met King Henry IV and
asked if he could build a chapel there 1399 (OP p186)
De Araz, William, mentioned at the end of the forestalling inquisition
1291 (LTH p17)
De Barton, Henry, collecting customs of wool 1331 (LTH p37)
collecting customs of wool 1332 (LTH p37)
De Barton, John, to collect prisages and customs in Ravenserod 1325
(LTH p37) collecting customs of wool 1325 (LTH p37) collecting
customs of wool 1332 (LTH p37)
De Bradele, John, burgess and merchant remonstrating to parliament
about piracy by Holland 1310 (OP p155) merchant mentioned at the
end of the forestalling inquisition 1291 (LTH p17) wool and hides
belonging to him 1321 (RO p26)
De Braddele, William, given protection to take goods to Newcastle and
Berwick for the king 1334 (RO p33)
De Bolebek, carucate of land in Ald Ravenser, no date given (OP p182)
De Cabhorn, manucaptor for Peter ate See as M.P. for Ravenser 1304
(LTH p23)

De Cakhowe, (Cackhow), Walter, burgess and merchant remonstrating to parliament about piracy by Holland 1310 (OP p155) wool and hides belonging to him 1321 (RO p26) granted protection to go to various parts of the country to source food 1316 (RO p29)

De Cathone, Walter, mentioned at the end of the forestalling inquisition 1291 (LTH p17)

De Collingham (Cottingham), John, rector of Easington church, received Easter offerings from 50 residents of Odd, no date given (OP p270) induced to resign the living of Easington 1339 (LTH p46)

De Coppendale, Adam, collecting customs of wool 1330 (LTH p37)

De Cotes, Hugh, merchant of Ravenser accused of forestalling 1290 (LTH p15)

De Cotes, John, granted protection to go to various parts of the country to source food 1316 (RO p29). Also had daughters, Margaret and Catherine, who left property at Winestead to Richard Ferriby (GP Vol 2 p537)

De Cotes, Robert, mentioned at the end of the forestalling inquisition 1291 (LTH p17) another Robert De Cotes? mentioned as staying on in the town after 1347 flooding (RO p19)

De Cotes, Thomas, died 1344-5, custody of all the lands and tenements he owned given to John de Monte Gomery and Roger de Munketon of York (LTH p55)

De Courcy, Ingelram, and his wife, Isabel, forfeited a place in Ravenser because of their defection from the cause of Richard II 1379 (LTH p56) had manor and hamlets there 1379 (OP p177)

De Crull, John, mentioned at the end of the forestalling inquisition 1291 (LTH p17)

De Doncaster, Richard, and Juliana, his wife, both of Ravenserhod, absolved from communication with Scots 1321 (LTH p27) delivered corn and salt to Scotland for the king, and further supplies for the Prince of Wales 1304 (RO p32)

De Drax, John, priest, mentioned at the end of the forestalling inquisition 1291 (LTH p17)

De Ferby (Ferriby), William, owned a ship of Ravenserodd called La

Saynte Marie, required by the king 1333 (OP p208) owner of the ship Margaret, said to be the best in Ravenser Odd, to proceed to Scotland 1335 (RO p33)

De Fortibus, William, (there were three of them) lord of Ravenser and Odd, earl of Albemarle and Holderness (OP p130) gave a parcel of land for the construction of warehousing suitable for herrings and other fish (OP p132), William II had three sons whom all died single (OP p280) (LTH p11) No dates are given. This is probably another spelling of De Forz (see below)

De Forz III, William, count of Aumale, gave half an acre in town to Meaux abbey between 1241 and 1249 (LH p211) granted by the king a weekly market and a September fair of 15 days in his manor at Ravenser Odd 1251 (LH p212)

De Forz, Isabella, countess of Aumale, wife of William, after her death in 1293 her attorney claimed jurisdiction over her tenants in Ravenser, also claimed the assizes of bread and ale, pillory, tumbrel, gallows, infangthef, and the rights of the sacrabar (LH p213)

De Glaumuill (Glanville), Hugh, rector of Easington church (LTH p46) loss of revenue when Ravenser under threat from sea 1347 (OP p174)

De Hill, William, mentioned at the end of the forestalling inquisition 1291 (LTH p17)

De Kyngeston, James, instructed to arrest three ships at Ravenser Odd for the king's service 1335 (RO p33)

De Langedik, Sir William, chaplain of St. Mary's Chapel, mentioned in Alexander Cock's will 1327 (ROLEYT p152)

De la Pole, Michael, earl of Suffolk 1326, eldest son of Sir William (OP p163) Ravenser Odd's most illustrious and well known family name.

De la Pole, Richard, the king granted dues and customs of the ports of Kingston upon Hull and Ravensrod to him 1326 (OP p160) collecting customs of wool 1325 (LTH p37) became mayor of Hull in 1320 (RO p21)

De la Pole, William, rich merchant and celebrity, (son of William), lent many thousands of pounds to King Edward III (OP p163), appointed commissioner and manager general of the Exchanges 1335 (OP p164) became first mayor of Hull (OP p165) given manor of Burstwick by the king 1356 (OP p237) selecting ships and men for the king's service 1335 (LTH p32)

De Mari, Peter, (Peter de la Mer?) merchant of Ravenser accused of forestalling 1290 (LTH p15) mentioned at the end of the inquisition 1291 (LTH p17) died 1318 -19 (LTH p51) also Att See?

De la Twyer, William, Seignorial Sheriff of Holderness, spent two days at Ravenser in 1263 dealing with troubles at sea (LH p75) seized a ship, and confiscated goods of some Hull merchants in 1265 (LH p212)

De Lythnay, William, of Ravensredde, victim of piracy 1346 (OP p270)

De Newton, Stephen, executor of the will of Alexander Cokes 1327 (ROLEYT p152)

De Ottele, Nicholas, chaplain at Ravenser Odd in 1311 (RO p20)

De Patrington, Stephen, mentioned at the end of the forestalling inquisition 1291 (LTH p17)

De Paul, Hugh, merchant mentioned at the end of the forestalling inquisition 1291 (LTH p17)

Derman, son of Walter, merchant mentioned at the end of the forestalling inquisition 1291 (LTH p17)

De Ravenser, John, involved in inquisition to establish the age of John atte See 1333 (RO p20)

De Ravenser, Matthias, mentioned in a Pipe Roll of 1230 and a grant of half a carucate of land in Ravenser in 1240 (SP p82)

De Ravenser, Odo, mentioned in a Pipe Roll of 1230 and a grant of half a carucate of land in Ravenser in 1240 (SP p82)

De Ravenser, Richard, Provost of Beverley in 1360, had a license from King Edward III to impropriate the church of Welwick (A History of Withernsea, Miles & Richardson p227)

De Ravenser, Roger, son of John, born 1311, became a merchant who sailed to Gascony in a ship called La Rose with herrings and other goods and to bring back wine 1336 (RO p20)

De Rison (Risum), John son of Ingram, held two carucates of land at Ravenser in 1285 (LTH p13) and also in 1303 (LTH p54)

De Seleby, Walter (son of Ralph), merchant of Ravenser accused of forestalling 1290 (LTH p15)

merchant mentioned at the end of the inquisition 1291 (LTH p17)

De Seleby, Margery, related to above (widow?)? taxed 6s 6d in 1297, so fairly prosperous (RO p19)

De Selby, Cecily, related to above? lost property in Odd due to floods 1347 (RO p19)

De Siwardeby, Robert, appointed in Ravenser Odd to ensure the masters and ships in the port joined the Admiral of the Fleet 1326 (RO p32)

De Skardeburgh, Alan, mentioned at the end of the forestalling inquisition 1291 (LTH p17)

De Stamelmere, burgess and merchant remonstrating to parliament about piracy by Holland 1310 (OP p155)

De Steeton, Robert, bailiff of Le Hod, foreign receipt from him 1261 - 64 (LH p229)

De Sterneton, Robert, to appear on behalf of Ravenser at a council at Westminster 1337 (OP p141)

De Thorp, Stephen, carucate of land in Ald Ravenser, rent given to Meaux abbey (1235 – 1249), also had son of the same name (OP p181)

De Welwyk, Peter, manucaptor for Thomas le Taverner as M.P. for Ravenser 1326 (LTH p23)

Del Hulle, William, manucaptor for William Pailleleve as M.P. for Ravenser 1304 (LTH p23)

Del Ward, Henry, mentioned at the end of the forestalling inquisition 1291 (LTH p17)

De York, William, to appear on behalf of Ravenser at a council at Westminster 1337 (OP p141)

Eren, Hugh, mentioned at the end of the forestalling inquisition 1291 (LTH p17)

Fitz Dien, Richard, collecting customs of wool 1332 (LTH p37)

Fhys, Roger, mentioned at the end of the forestalling inquisition 1291 (LTH p17)

Friboys, Beatrice, widow of Geoffrey, held half a carucate in town 1240 (Victoria County History, Vol 5, p69)

Galt, Thomas, mentioned as having plots in Odd, Alexander Cock's will 1327 (LTH p39)

Gril, Richard, mentioned at the end of the forestalling inquisition 1291 (LTH p17)

Hautayn, John of Ald Ravenser, knight's fee and land holding (GP Vol 1 p61 and p66)

Hildyard, Robert, bailiff to countess of Aumale, taking tolls of ships and their goods, no date given (LH p211)

John, the clerk of St. Mary's chapel, mentioned in Alexander Cock's will 1327 (ROLEYT p152)

Keling, Hugh, mentioned at the end of the forestalling inquisition 1291 (LTH p17)

Kelyng, John, owner of the ship Eleyne, of Ravenser, granted safe conduct to Scotland by the king 1339 (LTH p36)

Knote, Hugh, mentioned at the end of the forestalling inquisition 1291 (LTH p17)

La Barbur, Matilda, murdered at Ravenser in 1250s (LH p116)

Le Bucher (Butcher), Roger, mentioned at the end of the forestalling inquisition 1291 (LTH p17)

Le Chuffour, Gilbert?, M.P. for Ravenser 1327 (LTH p23)

Le Flekmaker, Hugh, occupied a plot of land on the king's soil and built a messuage there, later came into the possession of Laurence Lyggeard 1313 -17 (RO p19)

Le Ledebeter, Richard, master of the ship Faucon 1334 (RO p32)

Le Serjeant, Richard, mentioned at the end of the forestalling inquisition 1291 (LTH p17)

Le Stater, John, owned a load at Hull of wheat, hides, wool and tallow for export to France 1321 (RO p26)

Le Taverner, Hugh, collecting customs of wool 1330 (LTH p37)

Le Taverner, Richard, mentioned at the end of the forestalling inquisition 1291, steward of Beverley (LTH p17) given protection to take goods to Newcastle and Berwick for the king 1334 (RO p33)

Le Taverner, Thomas, member of parliament 1326 and again 1328 (OP p141) petition regarding his will mentioned in the reign of Edward III

(LTH p51)

Le Whyte, Peter, mentioned at the end of the forestalling inquisition 1291 (LTH p17)

Lygeard, Laurence, rented a property from Alexander Cokes in 1327 (LTH p55) came into possession of a property from Hugh Le Flekmaker 1313 -17 (RO p19)

Maletek, Roger, delivered corn and salt to Scotland for the king, and further supplies for the Prince of Wales 1304 (RO p32)

Marmion, Roger, rector of the church of Easington, involved in annexing the chapel of Ravenser Od, 1273 (OP p133)

Morkel, Matilda, owned one cottage, with appurtenances in Ravenser, died 1327-8 (LTH p55)

Morkel, Maud, involved in property dispute 1317 – 21 (RO p19)

Morkel, John, a bastard, see above dispute 1317 – 21 (RO p19)

Pailebone (Pailleleve or Payleve)), Walter, lost his appointment as coroner in Yorkshire because he now stayed continually in Grimsby 1341 (RO p43)

Pailebone (Pailleleve or Payleve)), William, one of the first members of parliament from Ravenser Odd 1304 (OP p141) granted protection to go to various parts of the country to source food 1316 (RO p28)

Prest, Gilbert, (Gilbert the Priest?) mentioned in Alexander Cock's will as having a tenement at Ravenser 1327 (ROLEYT p152)

Pyngel, Walter, mentioned at the end of the forestalling inquisition 1291 (LTH p17)

Reedbarowe (Reedbarrow), Richard, hermit at Ravenserporne, desired to build a lighthouse 1428 (OP p192)

Richard of Ravenser, archdeacon of Lincoln 1368 – 1386 (The Ravenser Composition p26) see Richard De Ravenser

Rose, John, mentioned at the end of the forestalling inquisition 1291 (LTH p17)

Rose, William, mentioned at the end of the forestalling inquisition 1291 (LTH p17)

Rottenherring (Rotenheryng), the surname is derived from the Germanic name for the red herring. Robert, to carry provisions for the

English in Scotland 1338 (OP p211), celebrated local family in town (LH p218) King Edward III granted safe passage to his ship, Radegunde in 1338 (LTH p53)

Rotenherying, John, leading merchant of Hull with family connections in Ravenser Odd, no date given (RO p21)

Scott, William, son of Bernard, given letter of attorney 1334 (GP Vol 2 p534)

Shail, Richard, mentioned at the end of the forestalling inquisition 1291 (LTH p17)

Taverner, Helen (surely a Le Taverner), present at the baptism of John ate See 1311 (RO p20)

Thorpe, Stephen, of Welwick Thorpe, probably the grandson of De Thorp, Stephen (see above) held a carucate and a half of land in Ald Ravenser 1344 – 5 (LTH p55)

Togge, John, bequeathed a tenement in Ravenser Odd to Catherine, his wife, and Alice, his daughter 1334 (LTH p55)

Trenthemer (Trenchemer), John, burgess and merchant remonstrating to parliament about piracy by Holland 1310 (OP p155) cargo freighted to him 1320 (RO p26)

Trewe, Gilbert, mentioned at the end of the forestalling inquisition 1291 (LTH p17)

Trunk (Trunck), Richard, burgess and merchant remonstrating to parliament about piracy by Holland 1310 (OP p155) owned a load at Hull of wheat, hides, wool and tallow for export to France 1321 (RO p26) delivered corn and salt to Scotland for the king, and further supplies for the Prince of Wales 1304 (RO p32)

Wyt, John, (Witte, White), member of parliament 1326 and again 1328 (OP p141) mentioned at the end of the forestalling inquisition 1291 (LTH p17)

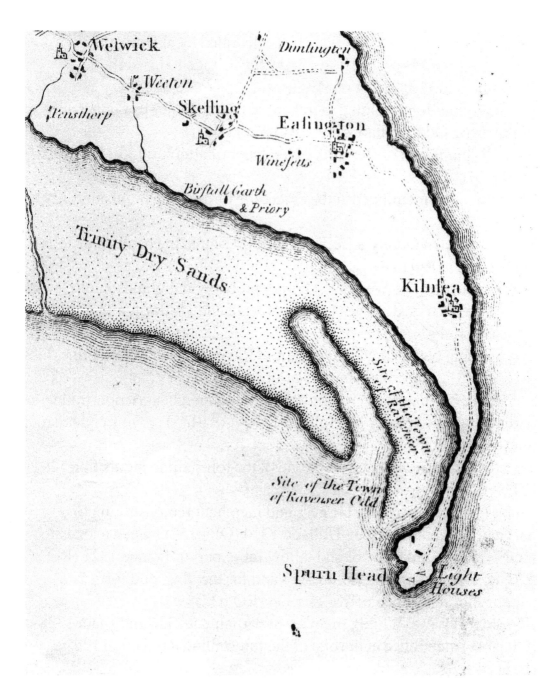

Tuke's map of 1786, where he clearly marks the 'Site of the Town of Ravenser Odd'.
Note the bulge on the left of the point, towards the present site of the Old Den. The
'Site of the Town of Ravenser' is also marked, but I suspect that the town was actually
much further east, and now under the North Sea. The lighthouses shown were built by
John Smeaton in 1776, and were over a mile south of the 1674 Angell's light.

The end of the town

As we have read, the initial grant of quayage was in 1296, but for a direct reference to the seriousness of the situation we need look no further than the year 1310, when, on October 6th at Biggar, the borough sought a 'Grant, for a term of two years, to the bailiffs and good men of the town of Ravensere, of murage for the repair of their quay, overthrown by the violence of the sea.' (CPR Edward II, 4 [1307 – 1313] Vol 1 p281) Apparently a complaint was received in 1313 that the money had not been used for this purpose. (RO p36, CPR 1307 – 1313 p67) Even so, there was a four year grant made to the port in 1315 for the improvement of the quay. (RO p27, CPR 1313 – 1317 p273) Further assaults by the waters continued, but it was not until the 1330s that things became serious, although one source suggests that in 1329 King Edward III struggled to obtain a list of burgages in the town, apparently due to 'the ruinous state of the town.' (DDCC / 41 / 3) Grants of quayage for the port continued until 1347. (VCH Vol 5 p68) The six grants made between 1296 and 1331 are listed as being for the town of Ravenser, but the remaining four after that date are for the town of Ravensrode. (LTH p18) The Chronicles of Meaux for the dates between 1339 and 1349, when Hugh of Leven was abbot, describes the situation;

'At that time the chapel of Ravenserre, dependent on the said church of Esyngton, recently appropriated to us and the greater part of the buildings of the whole town of Ravenserre, by the inundations of the waters of the sea and of the Humber, increasing more than usual, were almost completely thrown down. For which cause some inhabitants and dwellers in that town have removed to other places, leaving the said town in a measure desolate; so that the profits, tithes and offerings, which used to pertain to the said chapel, and in which the greatest part of the profits of the said church of Esyngton used to consist, on account of the absence of people, are to a large extent not forthcoming.' (LTH p47, CM iii p21)

There was a commission held on May 3rd 1343 to enquire and certify for the king whether it was true that the sea had indeed done much damage at Ravenser Odd. It was alleged that the site was so inundated that the tenants could make no profit there, and that the king's plots of land farm-let had been thrown down. Furthermore, it was stated that without the king's help, the townsmen were unable to save their houses, and so timber was needed for this and to repair the quays. (RO p36, CPR 1343 – 1345 p217) Action soon followed, for the keeper of the Forest beyond Trent, or his deputy in the Forest of Galtres near York, were ordered to have 500 oaks cut down, stripped and delivered to the stricken town as a gift of the king. It was acknowledged that great damage had been done at Odd, to its houses and quays, and that the loss of the town would be a significant loss to the area. (RO p37, CCR 1343 – 1346 p184)

In March 1344, quayage was once more granted for four years, to make good the damage to the quay. (RO p37, CPR 1343 – 1345 p217)

On May 18th 1346 a writ was issued for an inquisition to take place during the summer. The men of the port claimed that they were so affected by numerous inundations of the sea that the major part of the tenements and soils had been destroyed and carried away. Therefore, many of those who had been able to pay the charges levied had left, and those who remained had not the means to pay. (RO p37, PRO C 145 / 156 / 6) Here is a record from this inquisition;

'Inquisition taken at Ravenserod on Thursday in the feast of St. Lawrence the martyr, in the 20th year of the reign of King Edward the third after the conquest, before Nicholas Gower, Amandus de Frothyingham, and Peter de Grimsby, appointed by the commission of the lord the king to inquire concerning the impoverishment and destruction of the town of Ravenserod in Holdernesse, in the county of York, by the flowing of the water of the sea often inundating the said town, and concerning all other circumstances, by the oath of Galfrid de

Redmar, Hugh de Hoton, Thomas de St. Martin, Stephen de Newton, John de Northorp, John Rolland, Roger Rolland, Nicholas de Thorn, Peter Percy, William Buk, Walter …… ese, and William son of Hugh de Hoton jurors; Who say upon their oath that two parts of the tenements and soil of the said town and more, by the flowing of the sea often inundating the said town, have been thrown down and carried away, and the said town by the flowing of the water aforesaid has been daily diminished and carried away. And they say that many men of the said town, who were accustomed before this time to bear the burdens contingent to the said town, have withdrawn themselves with their goods and chattels from the aforesaid town, because of such daily increasing dangers there, making an abode elsewhere, so that there does not remain there a third part of the men of the town aforesaid, with their goods, who are able at the present time in any way to bear the burdens in this way contingent to the said town, nor sufficient to pay or support the tithes, tolls, and other burdens hitherto assessed upon the said town, and due to be raised there. In witness of which the said jurors have fixed their seals to this inquisition.' (LTH p38 – 39, Inquisitiones ad quod Damnum, 20 Ed III No 23)

In January 1347 the taxers and collectors in the East Riding were ordered to re-assess the inhabitants of the town according to the value of their moveables, thus superseding the levying of the ancient tenth. (RO p38, CCR 1346 – 1349 p183) In May the king informed the taxers and collectors of the biennial tenth that Robert de Cotes and the inhabitants who remained in Odd were to be assessed at 100 shillings for that year, instead of the former £15. They had until Michaelmas to sue for the discharge of the residue. There followed a complaint from the residents that the taxers still charged the old rate, but the king confirmed in 1348 that the new rate applied. (RO p38, CCR 1346 – 1349 p322, p430) However, it would appear that the residents of Ravenser Odd were not above reproach. The enquiry revealed that former residents who had moved out, avoided paying tallage and other charges by staying away most of the year, then returned secretly for the time of fishing, that is, September, for the purpose of gain. They then went home with their profits, without allowing the residents to take anything, or contributing toward taxes. The king then ordered that none of these former residents were permitted to return to the town, unless they stayed there and paid their dues. If they did return, the king would take their houses and rents, keeping half himself, and giving half to the community. (RO p38 – 39, CCR 1346 – 1349 p209)

To address these concerns, a writ was forwarded to the collectors of taxes in the East Riding from King Edward III during 1347 or 1348;

'The king to collectors of Taxes, etc., Whereas recently we have learned by an inquisition taken at Ravenserod that the town has been daily diminished by the frequent inundations of the water of the sea surrounding the said town, the soil thereof in great quantity has been carried away; and that 145 buildings which belonged to Cecily de Selby, and very many which belonged to others, and forty two places not built upon which belonged to Thomas Galt and to others specified in the said inquisition, which said buildings and places constituted two parts and more of the aforesaid town, have been taken into the sea by such inundations, and the flux of the said water, from the 8th year of the reign of the king of England even to the day of the taking of the said inquisition; and that the persons who were accustomed to have and hold the said buildings and places, and to dwell in them, and thereof to bear the burdens attached to the same, have withdrawn themselves from that town by reason of such waste and the impoverishment thence arising; and that the persons now dwelling there are so impoverished that they are not able in any way to support and pay the tenths, tolls, taxations, etc. It is commanded that 100 shillings be accepted from the said inhabitants, for the said tenths, etc.' (LTH, p39, Rotulorum Originalium in Curia Scaccari Abbreviato ii, p188)

The Chronicles of Meaux abbey for the years 1349 to 1353 surprisingly do not mention the Black Death, which arrived at York in May 1348, and by summer, afflicted most of northern England. Meaux abbey finally succumbed in August 1349, when the abbot and 22 monks and 6 lay brothers died in the plague. Ultimately, only ten out of fifty monks and lay brothers survived. (RO p39, Philip Ziegler, The Black Death p180). Our island town would have had to contend with the inundations of the waters at the very time that many there were dying of this disease, and those who were ill had to be cared for by the few who were able. As a result of this, there was a chronic lack of labour to repair the jetties, quays and sea defences at this critical time.

At the same time that the burgesses of Odd were trying to get a reduction in their taxes, the monks of Meaux were making similar efforts to get a reduction in the tax of the mother church of Easington, which was appropriated to them in 1351 to compensate them for their losses. Apparently, Ravenser Odd's inhabitants had been the main source of the church's income. The income from tithes and other sources had been drastically reduced by the inundations within the parish, for the vills of Hoton, Northope, Dymelton and Newton were all suffering. The half an acre that the abbey owned in Odd, and also the chapel, had been laid open to destruction 'the said floods and inundations of the sea, as was their custom, welling up every fifteen days, foretelling the destruction of the town within a year before it happened, sometimes rising beyond measure higher than the town and like a wall encircling it on all sides.' (RO p40, Papal Letters IV p217) On the diminution of the revenue of Easington church, the chronicler of Meaux has this to say;

'and to what tax it was taxed, and also concerning the burdens incumbent on the said church, and concerning all other articles and circumstances, learned that the said church of Esyngton was taxed at 40 pounds a year; but that on account of the diminution and loss of the town of Ravensere Odd, as has been aforesaid, and of the towns of Hoton, Northorp, Dymelton and Newton, which were in and of the parish of the said church, consumed by degrees by the inundations of the sea in those parts, the profits of the said church of Esyngton, arising

from the marshes of the town of Esygnton, and from a place which is called "le Hawenne" (i.e. the haven), and other yearly fruits pertaining to the said church, have been daily diminished by the said inundations, and may be feared continually to diminish in a similar way in the future; and that the said church was perpetually burdened by yearly pensions, paying 38 marks (approximately £25) to various persons in ordinary burdens, besides finding one priest there, and other extraordinary burdens; and, by this means, all fruits, rents and yearly profits of the said church remaining in our hands, and to be converted to our use and advantage, with the necessary burdens of that church deducted, after the destruction of the town of Ravensere Odd, and other injuries effected by the inundations of the sea and of the Humber, scarcely amounted to 20 marks a year (approximately £13)...'
(LTH p49, CM iii p123 – 124)

As mentioned elsewhere, commissioners were appointed to view the banks of the region, including one as late as 1353 to oversee the Hull to Ravenser section. (OP p177 & 243) It would appear that the River Humber was evolving is such a way that in 1357, the tides were recorded as being four feet higher than usual, which resulted in the Hull to Anlaby road being raised six feet due to flooding. (OP p176 & 219)

By this time, the inhabitants of the town were gathering up such relics, crosses and other church ornaments as remained in their private possession, and were leaving the town to its fate. Initially, they settled at Drypool, but the lords of fee kept them waiting so long for an answer to their request to settle there that they decided to move on to Hull and other neighbouring towns, including Grimsby. (RO p41, CM iii p6, 16, 120) The chronicler of Meaux, writing between the years of 1356 and 1367, expounded it as follows;

'But in those days, the whole town of Ravensere Odd, in the parish of the said church of Esyngton, from the inhabitants and dwellers whereof the greatest part of the profits of the church of Esyngton used to arise, was totally annihilated by the floods of the Humber and the inundations of the great sea; and, by this cause, the tithes, fruits, rents, and profits of the said church of Esyngton were diminished to the amount of 50 pounds sterling in each year. And, when that town of Ravensere Odd, in which we had half an acre of land built upon, and also the chapel of that town, pertaining to the said church of Esyngton, were exposed to demolition during the few preceding years, those floods and inundations of the sea, within a year before the destruction of that town, increasing in their accustomed way without limit fifteenfold, announcing the swallowing up of the said town, and sometimes exceeding beyond measure the height of the town, and surrounding it like a wall on every side, threatened the final destruction of that town. And so, with this terrible vision of waters seen on every side, the enclosed persons, with the reliques, crosses, and other ecclesiastical ornaments, which remained secretly in their possession, and accompanied by the viaticum of the body of Christ in the hands of the priest, flocking together, mournfully imploring grace, warded off that time their destruction. And afterwards, daily removing thence with their possessions, they left that town totally without defence, to be shortly swallowed up, which, with a short intervening period of time, by those merciless tempestuous floods, was irreparably destroyed. But those inhabitants coming to construct and build there a suitable place for their merchandise, at Drypule, across the river of the water of Hull, in the parts of Holdernesse. But the lords of that fee not giving to them, at their will, speedy and placid consent, the said inhabitants determined to remove to that town of Kyngeston, and to other boroughs and maritime towns, wheresoever the spirit should lead them.' (LTH p40 - 41, CM iii p120 - 121)

The last mention of any commercial activity in the port is in 1358, when ships from the port were required to take wool from Boston. (UDDB / 3 / 1 / 7, CPR Edward III, 1358 – 61, 91) The last record of any activity at all was in 1362, when an act of vandalism occurred in the stricken town. As we shall see in a subsequent chapter, the record of this crime helps us ascertain the event and date of the town's demise.

The Chronicler of Meaux knew where to put the blame firmly for the port's obliteration, for Abbot Burton wrote of the period of William of Dringhow's first abbacy (1349 to 1353);

'When the inundations of the sea and of the Humber had destroyed to the foundations the chapel of Ravenserre Odd, built in honour of the Blessed Virgin Mary, so that the corpses and bones of the dead there buried horribly appeared, and the same inundations daily threatened the destruction of the said town, sacreligious persons carried off and alienated certain ornaments of the said chapel, without our due consent, and disposed of them for their own pleasure: except a few ornaments, images, books and a bell which we sold to the mother church of Esyngton, and two smaller bells, to the church of Aldeburghe. But that town of Ravenserre Odd, in the parish of the said church of Esygnton, was an exceedingly famous borough, devoted to merchandise, as well as many fisheries, most abundantly furnished with ships and burgesses amongst the boroughs of that sea coast. But yet, with all inferior places, and chiefly by wrong-doing on the sea, by its wicked works and piracies (praedationibus), it provoked the wrath of God against itself beyond measure. Wherefore, within the few following years, the said town, by those inundations of the sea and of the Humber, was destroyed to the foundations, so that nothing of value was left.' (LTH p47, CM iii p21, RO p39 – 40, CM iii p79)

Incidentally, this was not the only place to disappear at the time, allegedly due to an act of God. The town of Winetha in the Netherlands was washed away by the Baltic 'because of its sins', so that no trace of its existence remained (THT p23).

The old township of Ravenser lived on after the destruction of Odd, for it is still mentioned in 1379 as having manors and hamlets held by

Ingelram de Courcy, and even as late as 1397, Ald Ravenser paid rent to Meaux. (OP p177 & 181). It would seem that it did not survive much beyond that date. I have been unable to ascertain whether the old town vanished due to coastal erosion from the east or inundation from the Humber from the west, or a combination of both. However, in the surreal realms of government bureaucracy, the final nail in the coffin of the 'new' town of Odd took place much, much later, for administratively, it was not until 1835 that The Municipal Corporations Act finally deprived Ravenser Odd of its municipal officers! Only then was the town expunged from interference from the state. (NTMA p314)

After the flood

After the town was inundated in 1362, little of significance is mentioned of the place until June 1399, when Henry, duke of Lancaster, landed at a place called 'Ravenser Spurn'. King Richard was seen as weak, and Henry had returned from France to attempt to seize the crown. By September 30th, with an army of 60,000 men, he had achieved his aim, and became King Henry IV. That the place was at, or close to Ravenser can be deduced by the first part of the name. The word 'spurn' is suggestive of a spur or promontory. I believe that the two are actually one and the same place.

The town of Ravenser Odd was no longer recognizable as such, but I suggest that the site still existed as an island or gravel bank, perhaps washed over at the highest tides. To locals, it still was the place called Ravenser, at the end of that road which 'remains visible both to pedestrian and equestrian travellers; but its furthest part, for the space of half a mile, has been washed into the Humber since those days by the tides of the sea.' (LTH p11, from CM iii p121 - 122) The addition of the word Spurn is used to differentiate it from the well known town no longer in existence, even though it was located in approximately the same place. To reinforce this view, I can do no better than quote abbot Burton's successor as the scribe of the Chronicles of Meaux, for he twice mentions the landing at this place of Henry IV. In one place he writes of him 'landing at Ravenser Spurne' (LTH p57, CM iii p299). Elsewhere he expands on this by saying he landed 'at the aforementioned place called Ravenserodd, where the aforementioned but then consumed town of Odd near Ravenser was built long ago.' (LTH p57, CM ii p254) This appears to be pretty conclusive that they are one and the same site. Additionally, in the Hedon inquisition of January, 1401, the chapel of Ravenserodde, with the town itself, was declared to be worth, in spiritualities, more than £30 per annum (LTH p 49). This suggests that although the town and its revenues had gone, some part of its estate still existed, and that this continued to be a source of revenue.

We now turn to the singular chap who met the future king as he disembarked at Ravenser Spurn in 1399. This fragment of vulnerable 'land' if we may call it that, had gained a hermit called Matthew Danthorpe. The future king was so impressed by this good omen, that a day after he was declared sovereign, he granted a royal license to Matthew to continue and complete the hermitage and chapel which he had already started. Here is the substance of that decree;

'The king, to all to whom, etc, greeting.'
'Be it known that, whereas Matthew Danthorp, hermit, has begun to build a certain chapel, in a certain place called Ravenserespourne, at which, at our last coming into England, we landed (our license herein not being obtained), which he intends, as we have learned, to complete, at his great cost and expense, for the love of God and of the blessed Virgin Mary, in whose honour the aforesaid chapel, so begun, is to be built, and also that the said Matthew may attain a more joyful and fervent mind for the completion of the said chapel, of our special grace we have pardoned and remitted to the said Matthew, all manner of trespasses and mistakes committed by him in this matter, and whatsoever is forfeited by him into our hands, or incurred by the said aforesaid occasions.
And moreover, of our more abundant grace, we have given and granted to the said Matthew the aforesaid place, to hold to his successors, the hermits of the aforesaid place, together with the chapel aforesaid, when it shall be built and finished, and also the wreck of the sea, and waifs, and all other profits and commodities contingent to the sands for two leagues round the same place, for ever
Saving and reserving always to the chief lord of that fee the royal fishes, which may there be found: The statute passed concerning placing lands and tenements in mortmain, or any other cause whatsoever, notwithstanding. In which, etc,'

'Witnesses by the king at Westminster, the first day of October. By the king himself.' (LTH p58 – 59, Rymer's Foedera viii, p89)

By 1427 - 28, Matthew had gone, and in his place was another hermit, Richard Reedbarrow. His ambition was to build a lighthouse, and he addressed a petition to parliament to that end. He was granted his patent, and here we read parliament's response:

'The king to all whom, etc, greeting. Know ye that whereas there exist divers places and dangers in the entrance into the river of Humbre from the sea, where many vessels, men and merchandise, are often unfortunately lost, and in danger as well by day as by night, for want of a certain mark called a "beken", by which people might know to hold the right channel; and a certain Richard Reedbarowe, hermit of the chapel of the Blessed Mary and St. Anne at Ravensersporne, having pity and compassion of the Christian people and of the goods and merchandise there lost, has charitably begun (to build) a certain tower there, for the preservation of the said Christian people, and of the goods and merchandise coming into the river, to be a mark visible and noteworthy by itself by day, and by light to be found in it by night, to all vessels coming into the same river, which tower, without great costs, to help and relief of sailors, mariners, and ships coming thither, cannot be perfected and brought to an end, as we are informed more fully by a certain petition laid before us in our present parliament, by the commons of our king of England, assembled in the same parliament; We, wishing, as we are bound, to provide everywhere for the preservation and security of our liege subjects, by the advice and consent of the lords spiritual and temporal, and at the special request of the commons aforesaid, have granted and given license to the mayor of Hull for the time being that he, for the ten years next ensuing, in aid of the completion and construction of the tower aforesaid, may take and have, by himself and his deputies whom he pleases to appoint to this duty, from every ship of the burden of 120 tons and more, coming from the sea into the aforesaid river, 12d; and from every other ship of the burden of 100 tons, so coming from the sea into the same river, 8d; and from every other vessel of less burden coming in the same way into that river, 4d; as often as such ships and vessels shall come from the sea into the aforesaid river, as is aforesaid; Saving to the lords and all others of our liege subjects their liberties and franchises previously granted to them; Provided always that the moneys so to be received from the ships and vessels aforesaid shall be applied and faithfully expended in the completion and construction of the tower aforesaid, by the supervision, direction and advice of John Tuttebury, Thomas Marchall, John Fitlyng, Robert Holme and William Robinson, merchants and mariners, of the town aforesaid; or of any others to be appointed to this duty by the Chancellor of England for the time being; and that the aforesaid mayor, during the term aforesaid, shall yearly render a faithful account before the above-mentioned persons so appointed, and to be appointed, of the moneys to be received by him and his deputies aforesaid, whenever he shall be duly required to do so by the same persons. In which, etc, to continue for the aforesaid ten years. Witnessed by the king at Westminster, the 28th day of November.' [1427] (LTH p60 – 61, Patent Roll 6, Henry VI, part 1, m6)

Our final mention of Ravenser Spurn in this chapter relates to the return of King Edward IV after fleeing to Holland. The year is 1471. Boyle, in his book 'Lost Towns of the Humber' gives a full translation from Holinshed's Chronicle, but here I am concentrating on the passage relevant to Ravenser:

'The same night following, a great storme of winds and weather rose, sore troubling the seas, and continued till the fourteenth day of that month being Thursday, on the which day with great danger, by reason of the tempestuous rage and torment of the troubled seas, he arrived at the head of Humber, where the other ships were scattered from him, each one seuered from other; so that of necessitie they were driuen to land in sunder where they best might, for doubt to be cast awaie in that perilous tempest. The king with the lord Hastings his chamberleine, and other to the number of fiue hundred men being in one ship, landed within Humber on Holdernesse side, at a place called Rauenspurgh, euen in the same place where Henrie erle of Derbie, after called King Henrie the fourth landed, when he came to depriue King Richard the second of the crowne, and to usurpe it to himselfe.

Richard, duke of Glocester, and three hundred men in his companie, tooke land in another place foure miles distant from thence, where his brother Edward did land. The earle Riuers, and with him two hundred men, landed at a place called Pole (Paull) fourteene miles from the hauen where the king came to land. The residue of his people landed some here, some there, in place where for their sureties they thought best. On the morrow, being the fifteenth of March, now that the tempest ceased, and euerie man being got to land, they drew from euerie of their landing places towards the king, who for the first night was lodged in a poore village two miles from the place where he first set foot on land, etc, etc' (LTH p62, from Holinshed's Chronicle, edition of 1808 iii, p303 - 304)

The poor village mentioned would be Kilnsea, it would not be Easington, which was somewhat more substantial and prosperous. Additionally, Easington was nearer to four miles from the site of Ravenspurn. The document continues to mention the king's progress to York, and his meeting with a certain Martine de la Mare, who one may reasonably assume was a descendant of the original Ravenser family of 'Att See'

This concludes our study of the period after the inundation of Ravenser Odd in the 1360s.

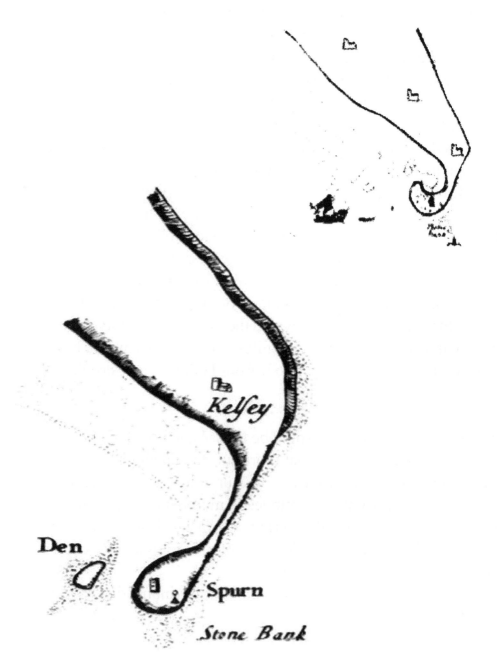

Kelsey

Den

Spurn

Stone Bank

The main image is from the Grenville Collins map of 1684. The survey was probably done when the tide was high, as the Old Den is clearly detached. The inset is a detail from the Scott map of 1734, and probably appears so hooked in shape due to a survey at low tide, when the Old Den was connected. Incidentally, the lighthouse shown in both maps is the 1674 Angell one, which was over a mile north of the present building.

What really happened to Ravenser

I will first look at the site's formation, before postulating what became of the town in the 1360s.

Old Ravenser was not recorded in the Domesday Book of 1086 (Frost's Notices relative to the early history of the town and port of Hull p54), and so the manor and its appurtenances probably came into being in the 12th century. As it was referred to as 'Old' when Odd came along in 1230, it would be reasonable to assume that Old Ravenser originated earlier rather than later in the 12th century. Prior to its establishment, it would appear that Kilnsea was the most southerly habitation on the tip of Holderness. Indeed, I believe that the location referred to as 'Hrafnseyr' (The raven's tongue or raven's sandbank), mentioned in the Icelandic Sagas was a wedge shaped prominence not far from Kilnsea. This was the occasion when King Harold saw the northmen off after the Battle of Stamford Bridge in 1066. The 'eyr' part of the place name denotes 'a narrow strip of land between two waters', and a very appropriate description for the area. Modern research on Spurn Point has postulated that there are two gravel ridges from the Ice Age under the peninsula which give it some stability (IECS 1992). The inner of these moraine ridges is located at the northern end of the Chalk Bank. In the light of the extensive gravel trade undertaken along the peninsula in the 18th and 19th centuries, I am confident that the material exploited was part of a glacial moraine that dated from the end of the last ice age. The district boasts another moraine, at Kelsey Hill, Keyingham, which was similarly exploited in the 19th and 20th centuries. I postulate that the cobbles of the coastal moraine were the backbone on which the road to, and the body of the town were to be built.

As the earliest descriptions of the road from Ald Ravenser describe 'a sandy road extended, covered with round and yellow stones' (LTH p11, from CM ii p121 - 122), we may assume that this could have been the northern of those ridges. Furthermore, as it was 'thrown up in a little time by the height of the floods', I offer the explanation that it was a storm surge that created the foundation for the town near the end of this particular ridge.

But which surge, and when? A prime candidate must be the first St Marcelus Flood of January 16th 1219. Even though the vast majority of the water in the Humber is derived from tidal inflow, the ebb tide, assisted by the additional fresh water from inland is somewhat stronger than the flow. If there had been much rain, the river would have been a raging torrent at full ebb, as the Humber drains one fifth of the whole of the area of England. I believe that in the wake of this storm surge, there was an accumulation of much silt and debris against the riverside edge of the cobble ridge that I have mentioned above. This natural 'warping' of the area between mudflat and the raised cobbles would not have passed unnoticed by the locals, who probably assisted this natural process by man-made means. Initially, they only dried nets on the site (GP Vol 2 p530), but by 1230 they decided to colonise this opportunity on their doorstep. As we know, there was a shipwreck at the location in 1231. The clue to the rise and fall of Ravenser Odd lies with the hydrographics of the River Humber. Changing river flows assisted in the creation of the island, if we may call it that, and they almost certainly explain its inundation in the late 14th century and eradication as a port. The well documented erosion of the Holderness coast was only a bit player in this particular drama. Here I introduce evidence from the very thorough treatise by William Shelford, written in 1869;

'But as the flood tide continued to wear into the Lincolnshire shore, so would the north or Ebb channel become weaker; until, being no longer able to transport the shingle thrown up by the sea, it would be closed by its rapid advance, and a neck would be formed, having the sand or island, upon which Ravenser Odd was afterwards built, for its southern termination.' (SOH p16)

Shelford believed that Spurnhead was in this state in 1250. That the river changes course, and that the deep navigable channels regularly alter, can be in no doubt. Indeed, the authorities frequently relocate the navigation buoys to define the safe channels for shipping. In relatively recent history, the early 19th century, Read's Island, near South Ferriby, was formed and people lived on it until the 1980s, when the river started to reclaim it. Whitton Sand, opposite Broomfleet Lock, was until recently described as a sandbank, but now is well above high tides, and with vegetation growing on there, it could be more appropriately described as an island. The most famous of all, is of course, Sunk Island, but more of that presently.

With modern eyes, we tend to superimpose the medieval town on the Spurn Point we know today. This seriously distorts the reality of what Ravenser Odd was probably like. Today at Spurn, we see sand dunes, some well over ten metres high, with little soil, and hardly any cobbles, except in certain areas. The present promontory, with its long gradual curve towards the west, is almost certainly not typical of any previous incarnations in this area. Firstly, it has had much interference from man, and groynes have protected it for over 150 years. This has also assisted in the lengthening of the site. Secondly, the sand has built up much higher at the point than has been true historically. Even one hundred years ago, the lookout post on the seaward side for the lifeboatmen was only a few metres above their cottages on the riverside. I believe that the spit that was the Odd was very different indeed. True, the land access was across a sandy road, but one that had many 'round and yellow stones'. On the beaches of Spurn today you will find little evidence of round yellow stones. In the next chapter you will find out why.

The historical mention of sand and cobbles has naturally led readers to perceive the town as built on sand. I think this extremely unlikely. As mentioned above, I consider that the cobble ridge acted as a natural dam that collected much debris, and not a little silt. This then rapidly warped up, and it was upon this 'new earth' that the merchants built their new town. How can we be sure that there was soil in the town? We know that there was a chapel in the town by 1272 (LTH p43, CM ii p153), which would have been on the highest point. Its raised prospect ensured that its destruction came about as late as 1355, when on July 25th, the abbot of Meaux was ordered 'to gather up the bodies of the dead which had been buried in the chapel yard of Ravenser, and which by reason of inundations were then washed up and uncovered, and to bury them in the church-yard of Easington. (LTH p47, CM iii p79) No ecclesiastical authority worth its salt would tempt the Almighty by contradicting the biblical instruction not to build on sand. The chapel and its graveyard were on earth; the church does not inter the dead in sand or shingle.

Furthermore, we have documentary evidence that the town was built on soil. Because there was so much damage done to the place, the residents were naturally unhappy at having to continue paying the tolls demanded of them as though nothing in the port had changed. As we have seen in a previous chapter, King Edward III addressed their concerns by issuing a writ in 1347 / 1348. It clearly states that the townsfolk were complaining about the bulk of 'the soil' being carried away.

'The king to collectors of Taxes, etc., Whereas recently we have learned by an inquisition taken at Ravenserod that the town has been daily diminished by the frequent inundations of the water of the sea surrounding the said town, the soil thereof in great quantity has been carried away.' (LTH p39, Rotulorum Originalium in Curia Scaccari Abbreviato ii, p188)

The final, and conclusive piece of evidence is that even as early as 1270, Odd had 'a little pasture'. (VCH Vol 5 p71)

Another aspect of the promontory that was radically different then was its shape. Early maps, though unreliable by modern standards, tend to show the peninsula in a much more hooked shape. Care must always be taken with charts of such an ephemeral location as Spurn, for the state of the tide when the cartographer mapped it can make a radical difference to details of the place. Bearing this in mind, we can still clearly see that the modern promontory curves round to point south west, whereas in some old maps the spit curved hard to the west from about Kilnsea Warren. This may help to explain why Ravenser Odd was in the parish of Easington, but Old Ravenser was in the parish of Kilnsea. Odd, though beyond Old Ravenser when travelling by land, was actually quite close, as the crow flies, to Easington. (See maps on page 82) There is support for this notion from Richard Potter's chart of 1584, when 'Hawke Road or anchorage' is marked inside the spit. De Boer considered that 'Hawke' was a corruption of 'Hook'. Indeed, in Dutch pilot books that appeared at this time, Spurn is called 'The Hook of Humber'. (UDDB / 3 / 1 / 7 p41)

Additionally, there is little evidence to suggest that the profile of the riverbank at Kilnsea was much different from today. In other words, the approach to the seaport by land was much broader in appearance. Whereas today there is less than a quarter of a mile between sea and river at Kilnsea Warren, in the 13th century, there would have been at least a mile at the start of the promontory, gradually narrowing down until it reached the cobble causeway that marked the approach to the port. Having thus presented a glimpse into Odd's creation, and studied some natural characteristics of the place, let us now turn our attention to the events surrounding its destruction.

It is appropriate at this juncture to give a historical overview of the climactic conditions at the time, taken from Hubert Lamb's excellent text – Climate, History & the Modern World. The 13th century was generally warm, and these conditions continued until about 1310. There then followed a number of extremely wet years with severe storms. From 1314 or 1315 until 1321 there were a series of disastrous harvests due to very cold and wet summers, and starvation was rife. The weather overall in the 14th century was very unsettled, and 14 serious sea floods were recorded. There had only been 3 in the previous century, and only 4 were then to be chronicled in the 15th century. The prevalence of easterly winds at latitudes 50 – 55°N in the 14th century would also add to the discomfiture of a north eastern seaport like Ravenser Odd.

As to the timing of the port's destruction, with incredible irony, I believe that the second St Marcelus Flood of January 16th 1362, also called 'Grote Mandrenke' (The Great Drowning), was to be the final nail in the coffin of this once great town. A considerable portion of the Suffolk village of Dunwich was lost, and on the other side of the North Sea, the Frisian town of Rungholt vanished in the same storm surge. Why am I am confident that it was this particular storm that finally eradicated the port? Because of an interesting reference in the Easington manorial court rolls, dated January 31st 1362 (SH p83). We know that trade had ceased in the port in 1358 (SH p83, CPR 1358 – 61, 91). It was then a ghost town, a shell, left to its watery fate. The church had abstracted anything of value from St Mary's chapel, and it was probably already falling into ruin, the bodies having been re-interred elsewhere in 1355. With an eye to recycling, some enterprising individuals appeared before the court at Easington, charged with 'throwing down and rooting up the timber of the staithes at Ravensrod'. This was just a fortnight after the great storm! The waters of the estuary were reclaiming the land they had given 140 years before, and the survivors of the Black Death in the area were reclaiming what the waters left to help secure their precarious futures. Probably at the same time, any useable stones from the chapel also found their way into local houses and barns.

What conditions conspired to destroy the town on this particular date? It has been suggested that a rise in sea levels during the 14th century were responsible for the town's demise. There appears to be some confusion over this issue, with one source advocating a slightly falling level, as the world moved nearer the 'Little Ice Age', which started in the early 17th century. Another source postulates a steady rise during this period, but I think any change had only a marginal effect on the fate of the port. I am supported in this view by De Boer;

'Though a considerable part of the peninsula was swept away about 1360, not the whole was taken, and re-growth of its successor appears to have started fairly soon after, although rise in sea-level continued. Thus, this rise of sea-level, which had other effects in the Humber discussed by De Boer (1976, p11 -13), does not appear to have been of itself a sufficient cause of the disappearance of Ravenser Odd.' (DDB / 4 / 4 / 4 p14)

I believe that the circumstances were ripe for the town's end because the flows in the Humber were evolving in a way that was detrimental to the survival of the site. The port's lifespan was inextricably tied in with the creation and loss of several villages on the Holderness riverside – Sunthorp, Orwithfleet, Frismersk and Tharlesthorp. These lands, some now under the Easington and Skeffling Clays, and some under the present Sunk Island, were also coming into being about the time that Ravenser Odd appeared. Natural warping created the impetus for local folk to enhance and reclaim very fertile land, and so villages like Frismersk and Tharlesthorp came into existence, but were to scarcely outlive the great port's demise. I believe that the formation of these lands on the north side of the estuary at that time changed the character of the ebb of the Humber. Frismersk was not mentioned in the Domesday Book; its first mention is in the Chronicles of Meaux, 1210 - 1220, when it is entitled 'Frismarisco'. (Gordon Ostler – Lost villages of the Humber Estuary p13) A date so close to the emergence of Ravenser Odd is surely no coincidence. Drawing on Shelford once more;

'And when, moreover, the marsh banks had been restored and the accretions in the closed channel to the north, which were called "Freshmarsh", had formed, the high-water line in the upper reaches not only attained the sea-level, but rose above it. A depression of the low-water line followed, and thus, in the next century (1350), there might easily be an increase of 4 feet in the tidal range at Hull, if low-water mark was taken as the standard from which to measure, as it probably was. The increased range produced greater depth, and, consequently, greater velocity, and the position of Ravenser-Odd became rapidly weaker. Its mercantile population removed to Hull (about 1357), and, at last, the town was carried away altogether in 1360, leaving, however, a bank of shingle called Ravenspurgh, which might still serve as an excellent pier or landing-place to the then declining town of Ravenser; and on this Spur, or more likely in Ravenser itself, stood the cross supposed to commemorate the landing of Bolingbroke. The banks of Freshmarsh, and the marsh itself, were probably destroyed by the increased tidal scour, and by the greater force of the current of the flood tide which the alterations at the mouth might throw upon them.' (SOH p16 - 17)

That the local lords wanted to save Frismersk and its neighbours we know from repeated appeals for funds to repair the riverbank. Shelford again;

'In 1341 a Commission was appointed for viewing and repairing the banks on the coast of Humber in the towns of Patrington, Frismersh, Ottringham & etc; and again in 1343. In 1345 the charge of supporting the banks and sewers in Frismersh had become very burdensome, and the inhabitants petitioned the King that their lands were overflowed by the tides of the Humber.' (SOH p8)

This is reinforced by Boyle;

'In Edward III (1342 – 43), Ralph de Bulmere, John de Sutton, John de Meaux, Thomas de Burton and Thomas de Cayton, were appointed to view and repair the banks, etc, on the coast of the Humbre, in the towns of Frismersh, Tharlesthorpe, Kayngham, Ryel, Burton Pidse and Halsham. Two years later a similar commission, including, however, the banks on the sea coast of Holderness, was issued to Robert de Hilton, William L'engleys, John de Constable, of Halsham, and Walter Waldegrave.' (LTH p72)

Thus, we observe that the process of warping and land creation in the 13th century had gone into reverse in the 14th century. As seen from the reference above, William Shelford's study supports this view. However, Shelford appears to suggest that the warping of Frismersh and neighbours in the early 13th century ultimately created a threat to Odd, by narrowing the channel, and thus raising the tide levels. I would suggest that the opposite is more probable, that the extension of the shoreline southwards into the river helped silt up the northern channels of the Humber near Odd, much as the Kilnsea Clays are now very silted up. This would keep the deeper, more destructive waters away from the seaport. As can be seen from Boyle's map of the lost villages (See page 8), they tended to be in closer proximity to the peninsula than the present Sunk Island is, and so offered more tidal protection. When these reclaimed lands started to be engulfed, the shoreline receded, and brought the destructive currents closer to Odd.

Whichever view is taken, one can be sure that the life and death for Ravenser Odd was inextricably tied in with the life cycle of these vulnerable warp lands. Ultimately, man lost both the 'new' warp land and the 'new' town at the river's mouth. The same estuarine tidal forces nurtured, sustained and then destroyed them both as part of this natural cycle. Having washed over and decimated Ravenser Odd in 1362, the Humber was to eradicate other villages in south Holderness in quick order. Orwithfleet had already vanished in 1339, after suffering nearly 30 years of flooding. (LTOTYC p87) The dreadful storm of 1377 devastated Tharlesthorp, and by 1393 the whole site was lost. Frismersk hung on until 1396, when the Meaux Chronicles state the town 'totally lost, not a vestige of it is left'. (GP Vol 2 p528 – 529)

De Boer considered that Ravenser's demise was part of the 250 year cycle that he postulated for the Spurn peninsula. As such, he conjectured that the site was washed away completely, and lay under the waves, and that a new site, further west, would eventually be created by the natural processes of the sea. Modern theories dispute this. I quote from the study by Pye & Blott for the Aldbrough Gas Storage Project 'While there have undoubtedly been periods of breaching and shortening of the feature (Spurn), the evidence for self-limiting cyclical behaviour is limited. Borehole evidence suggests the neck of the barrier has moved only a short distance landward during the past few centuries. Back-barrier estuarine deposits are present beneath the landward side of the neck but do not outcrop on the seaward side providing no stratigraphic evidence for major barrier retreat.' In other words, there is no evidence to suggest that the present seaward side of the peninsula was formerly on the river side of an earlier point. There has been a shoreline in this area for a very long time, with little movement of the spit.

Therefore, the truth would appear to be more complex than De Boer's theory. Here we look at the Chronicles of Meaux abbey once again;

'Which road remains visible both to pedestrian and equestrian travellers; but its furthest part, for the space of half a mile, has been washed into the Humber since those days by the tides of the sea. Of the site therefore of the said town of Ravensere Odd scarcely a vestige remains.' (LTH p11, CM ii p121 - 122)

The text was written early in the 15th century, and the writer, Abbot Thomas Burton, states that 'scarcely a vestige remains'. Surely this means that the site could still be identified, and that remains, perhaps foundations, walls or staithes were then visible. Still in place was the road of cobbles that led to the famous town. In other words, this promontory was still in existence, but with nothing habitable at the tip.

In 1395, Robert Killingholme appeared before Easington manorial court, charged with 'taking stones away from Ravenser Spurn.' (UDDB / 3 / 1 / 7 p30, DHO 2 / 1 30 June, 19 Richard II) This is the first use of the new name for the spit, and the mention of 'Spurn', which like 'Odd' meant a projecting piece of land, or a spur. This court is again recorded in 1398 as lamenting the 'loss of the kay of Ravenser'. (UDDB / 3 / 1 / 7 p29, DHO 2 / 1 8 Oct, 22 Richard II) Additionally, the Meaux Chronicles record that at an inquisition held at Hedon on January 10th 1401, 24 messuages in Ravenserodd which belonged to the abbey, were still worth, besides reprises, £13 16s per annum. (LTH p41) Mention is also made of the town itself, which with spiritualities, was worth more than £30 per annum. (LTH p49) The resultant loss of revenue from the abbey's lands in south Holderness led to a dispute with Richard II to consider a partial exemption from the subsidy demanded by him at this time. (LTH p41) The town was gone, but there was still something of value within its boundaries in the broadest sense. Its presence was still to be felt however, for the town's remains were to be a hazard for shipping for a number of years. (Hull & East Riding Portfolio, volume 3, p75, CM iii p21, p79, p121)

From the first instance of the word 'Spurn' in 1395, it seemed to increase in usage as we move into the 15th century, for the sailing directions for the circumnavigation of England, written c1408, calls the place 'Spone'. (UDDB / 3 / 1 / 7 p31, Marine Cartography of Britain [Leicester University Press 1962, p23]). Old habits indeed die hard, for as late as 1423, the Easington manorial court had a defendant charged with taking sand from 'The Sporne', (UDDB 3 / 1 / 7 p31, Hull University Library manuscript DHO 2 / 1 20 June, 26 July 1 Henry VI) Obviously, the powers that be still clung to the notion that there existed value in the ravaged remains of the 'new town' which very rapidly had become an 'old town'.

Human habitation had been erased, but the tidal site lived on. Having briefly discussed the natural processes that created and decimated the promontory, let us now look in detail at the all important question – where exactly was this famous town?

Where exactly was Ravenser?

It becomes clear that despite its inundation, the site of Ravenser Odd was still extant in the late 14th century, although uninhabitable. As mentioned in the last chapter, the Chronicle of Meaux, written close to this time, makes it clear that 'a vestige remains'. (LTH p11, CM ii p121 - 122). Here I return to a pertinent observation in Boyle's 'Lost Towns of the Humber';

'The sands of Spurn have shifted, though not nearly to the extent commonly thought, and the present lighthouse does not stand on the site of its predecessors. But there is historic evidence that Spurn Head for many centuries has preserved the general outline it bears now, and which has been very aptly compared to the shape of a spoon.' (LTH p58)

This prescient comment anticipates modern theories by 100 years, but it is not literally true, as the spit has actually grown by a mile or more since Angell's lighthouse was constructed in 1674. De Boer's theory for the evolution of the point, presented in 1964, postulated that the spit, after destruction by the erosion of the North Sea every 250 years, 're-invents itself' at a new, more westerly location. This view has held sway for many years, but is now challenged by modern theories that suggest that there are parts of Spurn Point that are fixed by two ridges of glacial deposits (IECS 1992 p6 and Aldbrough Gas Storage Project 2010 Pye & Blott). With this in mind, consider the probable shape of the peninsula in 1400, derived from images in early maps. It curved sharply round south, then hard west, from its anchorage point near Kilnsea. Early maps of the Humber represent a spit that was much more of a hook than the more recent gentle curve to the south west (see maps on page 82). Ravenser Odd lay at the very tip of the western end of the spoon shaped hook, with the approach causeway often over-washed by the river Humber. Then, as now, the continual erosion of the Holderness coast brought debris down to the mouth of the river. At first, this just tended to 'thicken' the spit on its eastern side.

The name of Ravenser lived on after the landing of Edward IV in 1471 though, for it is included as a port in Leland's 'Itinerary' of 1538. 'From Kingeston to Patrington, where is an havenet or creke for ships, a X miles, on Humber shore on Yorkshire thens to Ravenspurg, the very point on York side of the mouth of the Humber, 10 miles.' (JL / 126 / 10 p313) It may have then been a safe berth, and sailors knew the area as 'The Haven' (LTH p49), but there is no mention of the place in the publication 'List of Ports and Creeks', written by Holinshed, who died in 1580. (LTOTYC p94) By this time the name Spurn was coming into more common use. The first chart to title the spit as such, and place it in its correct position was Angliae Figura, c1534 – 46. (UDDB / 3 / 3 / 3, De Boer & Carr, Early maps as historical evidence for coastal change p24) The nature of the promontory in the mid 16th century is made clear by a description written in 1567;

'Old Ravensey is wasted and by the sea consumed and worn away and the said Ravensey Spurn is a sandy hill environed and compassed about upon the sea side with the sea and on the other side with the Humber containing six acres whereupon is neither arable land meadow nor pasture, underwood nor trees neither anything else but only a few small bents and short scrubby thorns of a foot high not worth felling which Ravensey Spurn at ordinary spring tides almost overflown and of no value. Also there is another hill high adjoining the Ravensey Spurn called Conny Hill environed by the sea containing four acres which is neither arable land, meadow or good pasture woods underwoods not trees also no value. Moreover, the said Ravensey Spurn and Conny Hill are now in the tenure of Christopher Hilliard Esq as tenant at will and hath been in the tenure of his father and grandfather from time out of memory of man but by what title or estate the said Commissioners cannot certainly understand, and for the same he and they have paid the yearly rent of two shillings only.' (UDDB / 3 / 1 / 7, Hull University Library DDCC 139 / 70 p186)

From this description, it would appear that the site of Odd was on the river side, the western edge, of Ravensey Spurn, and that the eastern, seawards side, was now becoming a rabbit (conny) warren. As we shall see below, this sandy hill was ultimately to extend southwards and become the peninsula that we now know as Spurn Point.

That the promontory was little more than an elongated wedge is implied by William Camden's publication 'Britannia' of 1586, when he states 'On the very tip of this promontory, where it draws most to a point and is called Spurnhead, stands the little village of Kellnsey (SH p71). De Boer dismissed the notion that Kilnsea ever stood near the point, but as we know that Old Ravenser, which stood between Kilnsea and Odd was totally destroyed c1396 (GP Vol 2 p529), what other habitation is left between it and the mouth of the River Humber? None; south of the old village there was only Kilnsea Warren, and the spit as it curved sharply in towards the river. This view is further supported by no less than John Smeaton, who built the 1776 Lighthouse at Spurn;

'The spot of ground called the Spurn Point, seems to have undergone great changes; for in Camden's time, about a century before the petition for erection of lights, there seems to have been no more than a pretty sharp head of land, that did not extend far from Kilnsey, and was then called Spurn Head….' (Appendix to John Smeaton's Narrative on the building of Eddystone lighthouse, 2nd edition 1813, paragraph 332, p185 footnote)

We now continue into the 17th century. Over the years, the sandbank on the seaward side, which had only induced a thickening of the wedge, started to creep south and past the site of the ruined port. It was when this accretion nudged beyond the old site of Ravenser Odd (or Ravenser Spurn) that something happened. Robert Callis, Sergeant-at-law, in his readings, or Lectures on Sewers, delivered at Gray's Inn in the year 1622, says, that 'of late years parcel of the Spurnhead in Yorkshire, which before did adhere to the continent, was torn from there by the sea, and is now in the nature of an island (OP p20, SH p76, Callis p44). Also pertinent to this observation is the following passage;

'The local people who testified on behalf of the Constables in actions of 1684 and 1695 against the Angell family, declared that Ravensey Spurn had been swept into the Humber about 80 years previously, that what was left lay there, and that this, the little island in fact, rather than the new spit where the lighthouse stood, ought properly to be called Spurn or Ravensey Spurn. The place where the lighthouses stood was called Kilnsea Common or Point, or Gut-end (presumably because at that time the end of the spit was abreast of the little island and therefore of the southern end of the Greedy Gut, the stretch of water that separated the two). (SH p76 - 7)

This testimony is further expanded upon in De Boer's excellent response to the IECS report of 1992, entitled 'Spurn – Report of 1992, my rejoinder';

'Depositions in the 17th century law suits describe how Ravenspurn was breached, how the detached portion became an island which was later washed away completely, and how that part of Ravenspurn which was swept into the Humber by the formation of the breach developed into the island called by local country people Old Ravensey or Old Spurn Stones, and by seamen the South Point of the Humber, (the tip of the beheaded and shortened remnants of the spit was still called the North Point of the Humber), John Harrison's Hill, or Den. Though none of these sources gives the year of the breaching, the names Den and Den End are first recorded 1592 – 98 and again in 1608 – 16 in account books of the Hull Trinity House detailing payments made for setting up there of navigational beacons, actions no doubt necessitated by the changes brought about by these events at Spurn, and thus they suggest the period 1590 – 1610 for their occurrence. A reference in a survey of 1602 to 'the great wasting and decay of Ravenspourne' points to this period, as does a statement made by Hull Trinity House in

1618 that 26 or 7 years ago there was firm dry ground at Ravenspurne "but since then and now is utterly worn away and surrounded".' (UDDB / 4 / 4 / 4, p10 – 11)

De Boer took these two items to mean, as part of his 250 year cycle of the promontory, that it had become an island and was about to be washed away (see diagram on page 54). I read this passage differently. I believe that it was a 'parcel of land' that became an island, not the whole peninsula. That 'parcel of land', or 'the little island' as mentioned above, was actually the Old Den, the final vestige of Ravenser Odd, and the voracious waters created a channel between it and 'the continent' of The Spurn. The channel between them became known as 'Greedy Gut', which is an appropriate name for the insatiable hunger of the waters. One can easily imagine the local peasants and sailors conjuring up such a descriptive name for a stretch of newly created water.

There is further support for the above statement. On August 29th 1609, when James I granted the sale of land to Robert Angell and John Walker, the site purchased was called 'Ravensey' (DDCC / 41 / 3). As this was about the time that 'The Old Den' detached from the spit, it could well be that Angell & Co really bought into that remnant, and not the new promontory that was forming.

It is interesting, in the light of comments in the previous chapter about Ravenser Odd's fate being tied in with the villages of Frismersk and Tharlesthorp, which were near or under the present Sunk Island, that Sunk Island itself first appears on the 17th century maps as an island at the same time that the 'Old Den' first appears as an island. Could it be that once again flows in the estuary silted up the north channel, created warp land, and simultaneously turned the stub of the old promontory into this little island?

Now, let's look more closely at this place called the 'Old Den'. The place does not appear on maps until the 17th century. The name 'Den' for this new island first appears on a map of 1671. (UDDB / 4 / 4 / 4 p11) Thompson in his book 'Ocellum Promontorium' (OP p130) propounds that the location's name is derived from the Saxon 'den', a valley or dale. I am not confident that the local residents were familiar with the etymology of the Saxon tongue, and it is stretching the imagination to think that this islet looked like a valley. I suggest that what they saw was a new headland passing the 'old one', or should I say 'Old 'Un'. The 'Old Den' was the title that the 'olden' headland gained, and by 1675, the 'new' headland was now a sandbank stretching southwards past it. Thompson was singularly disingenuous if he thought that the Holdernessians derived an archaic Saxon word for one local feature, the 'Old Den' and the more prosaic term 'Greedy Gut' for the new channel that simultaneously created this new feature within the peninsula. It was at this time that the newly formed spit gained the title Spurn Point, for it is so named in the document 'Seller's – The Coasting Pilot'. (UDDB / 3 / 3 / 3, De Boer & Carr, Early maps as historical evidence for coastal change p26) The addition of 'Old' to the title 'Den' does not, however, appear on charts until c1770, by which time it was a degraded feature, over-washed at high tides. This erosion was almost certainly due to the lack of new sediment being transported there because the new peninsula that was now advancing south of it starved the feature of material. (IECS p22) I would suggest that its full title of 'Old Den' may have been in use locally for a considerable period before this date.

There is support for this overview of what was happening at Spurn from John Smeaton, the builder of the 1776 lighthouse. In the appendix to his work on the construction of the Eddystone lighthouse, he comments that this sandbank, south of the Angell lighthouse 'had afterwards become connected with the mainland, and so formed the Spurn Point of his day.' (SOH p7) In other words, the old promontory was left behind, a vestige, and the new accretion of sand and shingle crept past it on the eastern, seaward side, and became the Spurn Point that we now know, and where he built his guarding edifice.

Is the 'Old Den' really the site of the lost town? Boyle, writing in 1889, believed that the site of Ravenserodd was within the point, in the vicinity of the sand bank known as the Old Den (LTH p64). Here he concurred with Mr Tuke, who produced a map in 1786, placing the lost port near the Old Den (map on page 66). Boyle used some convoluted calculations with distances to arrive at this conclusion, and added further confusion by using statute miles instead of old English miles. Also, the Old Den is not a sand bank, it is a shingle ridge. Despite these flaws in his deduction, I feel that he was on the right trail. Interestingly, De Boer was also similarly inaccurate with his conversion of old English miles, for he stated that four 'old' miles were four and a half 'new' ones. (SH p82) It should read as five new miles, as an old mile was approximately ten furlongs and the new one is eight. Commentators have struggled over the distance quoted in the Meaux Chronicles (LTH p11, from CM iii 121 – 122) because taken literally, from say, Easington church, and travelling in a straight line, five miles would leave you standing on the very end of the present point! As we know that the spit has crept southwards by as much as a mile and a half since about 1600, something must be wrong. I believe that the answer lies in the hook shape of the old promontory, for to travel from Easington to Odd required a walk or ride around a long easterly arc that would now take you far out to sea before you approached the port from the east, not the north. (see the time line diagrams on pages 112 & 113) Even the boatmen who brought visitors across from Grimsby and Cleethorpes in the 19th and early 20th century believed Ravenser Odd to be on the site of the Old Den. A guide to Cleethorpes & Grimsby, published by Abel Heywood & Sons in 1909, states 'The voyager to Spurn Point (distance seven miles) will sail over the water which now covers the Port of Ravenserod, once a formidable rival to Grimsby.'

In 1912, Thomas Shepherd presented a different answer – Ravenser was to the east of the point (LTOTYC p94). His deduction was based on the continuous erosion of the Holderness coast. Extrapolating the present point back in history, at a rate of approximately two metres a year, one would arrive at a location about three quarters of a mile out to sea, and north of the present lighthouse. There is no doubt that the coast does erode, at varying rates, and it is easy to fall into the trap, as De Boer did, of assuming that a peninsula, similar in shape to the present one, behaved accordingly. Even John Smeaton fell into this trap;

'I had for some time considered the Spurn Point as an appendage to the high cliffs of Kilnsey; and formed from the waste of lands to the north; therefore, at whatever rate the sea encroached upon these cliffs, by taking off parallel screeds, this whole appendage of the Spurn must remove as an equal westward, upon the average.' (Appendix to John Smeaton's Narrative on the building of Eddystone lighthouse, 2nd edition 1813, paragraph 337, p188)

However, it would appear that this is not the case. With much more land to the north to protect it, the spit in Ravenser's day was considerably more sheltered from the destructive waves from the north. Research has shown that wave energy drops drastically as the angle of incidence falls. At Kilnsea, there is serious erosion, because the northerly currents dig deep into the north easterly facing boulder clays. As the peninsula sweeps southwards and then westerly, this energy, and its destructive force, drops away drastically. (Spurn Head, V J May, Geological Conservation Review, Vol 28 p6). Additionally, as I have endeavoured to demonstrate, Odd's promontory curved hard west, and into the Humber, so its fate was determined much more by the estuary's ebb and flow than the ravages of the North Sea. There is further support for this viewpoint in the Spurn Heritage Coast Study of 1992, 'as the shore bends to a south west alignment, the wave energy begins to decrease. The sediment carrying potential is therefore decreased and deposition takes place.' (IECS p26) The same source, on page 27, postulates that any south south east waves can cause erosion, but that they are less common at Spurn. This document also suggests that the feature known as 'The Binks', a long gravel bank on the seaward side of the point, protects it. 'The Binks themselves, in acting as a wave break for the spit, are clearly not a depositional feature or some form of Spurn relict feature, as has been held by some authors, but must have predated the development of Spurn.' (IECS p26) The Binks may indeed protect the present point, though I am not convinced that this long shingle bank predates the spit. Indeed, The Binks change all the time, for a strong northerly gale often removes most of the ridge. This is not to say that the point is not now vulnerable, for the rolling westwards of the area known as 'The Narrows', and the disappearance of much of the protecting Holderness coast at Kilnsea and Easington does now threaten its existence.

However, the reason that I believe that Boyle was on the right track with his location for Odd, is in the first hand evidence of local people. I give the reader two extracts, one from Thompson, and one ultimately from George Poulson's, The History and Antiquities of the Seigniory of Holderness 1840;

'Within the Spurn, is an oblique hollow place in the sand, of considerable extent, called the old Den and it has been supposed that Ravenspurne stood in or near the old Den; and some fishermen have asserted that they could see there, at low water in the Humber, fragments of walls, and other remains of buildings.' (OP p130)

'In digging some few years ago (this written circa 1840), on a place within the present Spurn Point called the Old Den, we found ashlar stone, chiselled and laid in lime; seemingly the foundation of some building of note; the heads of the piles also having been found. The Old Den is a singular ridge of gravel, full half a mile long, and not more than seventy or eighty yards broad, and raised about three feet above the mud banks by which it is surrounded. The shape of this ridge is half a circle, the open side facing the shore, and a channel, since my remembrance, between it and the shore, but the north-east end is now warped up. Thirty years ago the bay formed by this singular ridge was the best anchorage, for small vessels, in the Humber, and has been at some former period an excellent port'. William Child, Esq., of Easington, "a gentleman competent to give an opinion".' (LTH p64, GP Vol 2 p540)

Here we have, from two disparate accounts, evidence that there had been structures on the 'Old Den', a location, if some of the old charts are to be believed, near or upon the earlier hook shaped promontory. Additionally, Smeaton had this to say with regard to the Den's claim to be the site of Odd;

'There is also an obscure tradition current, that upon a flat of ground just within the point that now but just dries out at the low spring tides, there stood a considerable town called Ravenspurn; and some pretend they have seen traces of its foundations.' (Appendix to John Smeaton's Narrative on the building of Eddystone lighthouse, 2nd edition 1813, paragraph 332, p185 footnote) Incidentally, the word pretend, when used at that time, had the meaning of making a claim rather than the current implication of making something up.

Though I question De Boer's 250 year cycle for the point, a document of his, dated 1992, offers further support;

'Such a site might be where the head and neck would give protection from the sea and a feature analogous to the Den provide shelter from the Humber. Such a feature could have formed in the manner in which the 17th century Den formed but 500 years earlier, when the Ravenser Odd peninsula replaced an earlier spit.' (UDDB / 4 / 4 / 4 p12)

So have we at last located our legendary lost town of Ravenser? Perhaps. However I think the final solution may be still more complex.

Researchers tend to look to the east, or to the west of the spit, never underneath it. Here I introduce two articles by the well known naturalist and wild fowler, John Cordeaux, who knew the area very well. He wrote in 1892;

7. SUPPOSED SUBMARINE RUINS AT THE SPURN – Mr Winson, the well-known cockswain of the Spurn lifeboat, and a long resident at The Point, has recently given me the following information, which I took down at the time, on a matter which is well worthy of further investigation: - On the east, or seaside of The Spurn, about a quarter of a mile to the north of the lighthouses, there runs straight out from the coast a narrow bank called The Ridge, never uncovered at the lowest ebb by some feet. This bank runs N.W. to S.E. or directly out to sea: the place and direction are well marked, for on the calmest days there is always a ripple above it.

The ridge, one side of which drops comparatively into deep water, is neither sand or gravel or of native rock, of which, I need scarcely say, there is none to be found, but it is apparently composed of enormous stones, or perhaps masses of concrete with flat tops. Mr Winson has sounded over these with a boat hook, and been astonished at their great size. He thinks that the Ridge is in great part of artificial construction and not a bank or shoal cast up by the sea, the foundations rather of an ancient dockwall, mole, or breakwater, and, that from the direction it takes, it not improbably partly under-runs the so-called Spurn island.

On one occasion, Mr Winson and his crew went out to the assistance of a stranded fishing smack on the Ridge and got her into deep water uninjured, as she happened fortunately to rest for the time on the level surface of one of the great stones. Other evidence is also forthcoming, all tending to the same conclusion of the existence of ancient remains to the eastward of The Spurn.

The exact site of Ravenser and Ravenserodd has been matter of dispute, there can, however, be little doubt it was in the bay to the north-west of the Point, and is now marked by the bank called the Old Den. This, of mud and shingle mixed with fragments of brick, runs

parallel with the new chalk embankment and curves gradually inward towards the shore, nearly opposite to the 'Highbents'. It is the last portion of the mud flats covered by the tides, and I have seen the place at times crowded with various waders as they retreated before the rising waters: and now, as I write these lines of a former favourite fowling-place, I can imagine again the shrill 'cour-lie' of the restless whaup, the clear 'keep-keep' of the oyster catchers, the mellow 'louey-louey' of innumerable godwit, or the wilder 'chee-wheet' of the greenshank – but this is mere digression from my purpose. The question is, had this supposed breakwater, or whatever it was, presumably of Megalithic proportions, on the east side of The Spurn, any connection with lost towns of the Humber: or is it, more probably, of much more ancient construction, some relic of a Roman port or harbour within the river, and then situated considerably to the westward of its mouth? From what we know of the loss of lands on the coast of Holderness in historic times, this harbour, if it existed, would be completely protected to the north by a low range of hills, of whose western slopes the high lands of Dimlington and Kilnsea are the last relics. There are sound reasons for supposing the Romans had a port in the Humber between the mouth of the river and Brough, all traces of which may have been swept away at an early period by encroachments of the sea, and slight deviations in the river course, and these immense flat stones may possibly have some connection with the same. I hope in the course of next summer to be able to ascertain by sounding, the exact position and the extent of the Ridge, and its probable constructors.
Eaton Hall, Retford   John Cordeaux
(Lincolnshire Notes & Queries, Volume iii, No 17, January 1892)

63. THE SUPPOSED SUBMARINE RUINS AT THE SPURN – In a recent number of Lincs. N & Q, I drew attention to some indications of ancient construction in deep water, east of The Spurn. Since this I have had an opportunity, by the kindness and with the co-operation of Captain D E Hume, of the Humber Conservancy, of a preliminary examination of the so-called 'Ridge', east of the Point.

The time chosen was August 11th, at low water of one of the lowest ebbs of the year. The position is about three-quarters of a mile north of the High Light. From the foreshore the direction is very well marked by the ripple above the bank. How far the ridge extends eastwards is not known, but it must be a considerable distance. At the time of our visit there was five feet of water over that portion nearest the shore. The Ridge is undoubtedly artificial, steep to the north and sloping to the south. I was told that once during a northerly gale, a foreign vessel got inside the 'binks' and was driven on the edge of the ridge, sinking within a few minutes and entirely disappearing. Without a diver it is impossible to speak as to the character of the material used in construction: probably it is concrete, the large size of the presumed blocks, described by Mr Winson (Lincs. N & Q, p22), and gigantic character of the structure, point rather to concrete than stone as likely to be used by the original builders. Tried with a boat hook the summit feels like rock, and is to some extent honey-combed, the cavities being filled with gravel. The lead falls as on a pavement, and soundings to the north clear of the ridge shew a sudden drop to deep water.

In a chart of the Humber made by Lord Burleigh, temp. Elizabeth (1579), a ridge or bank is marked as running west to east outside The Spurn, and as true as if laid down by a rule. This is called the 'Stone bench', a term suggestive of a structure, recognised at that date, as made of stone or such like materials. This breakwater, dock side, or mole, whatever it may be, has undoubtedly a connection with some ancient port at the entrance of the river. After reading all that has been written by recent authors on the subject, I am fully convinced that it is an error to place the position of the lost towns of the Humber within the present point, and on the shoal known as the 'Old Den'. Sufficient allowance has not been made for the great physical changes which have taken place, and are still progressing, in the position, from century to century, of these shifting shores. The Spurn is a compromise between the tides of the North Sea and the re-flow of the Humber. And since about the middle of the 14th century, when Old Ravenser and Ravenser-odd were taken by the sea, probably, from what we know of the annual waste of this coast, between one and two miles of land have disappeared eastwards of The Spurn, and the point also has extended itself a very considerable distance to the South. In fact, the known southward extension from 1676 to 1875 is 2703 yards, or an average rate for 200 years of 13.5 yards per annum. The west-ward movement of the promontory also has kept pace with the waste of the coast to the northward. It is evident then that the position of the lost towns is somewhere at sea from one to two miles north-east of the present high light. A line drawn from Easington Church, N.W. to S.E. for four miles, and passing the site of Old Kilnsea and so out to sea, would probably touch the sites of Sunthorpe, Old Ravenser and Ravenser-odd.

It is not unlikely the stone ridge east of The Spurn may have some connection with these long-lost ports of the Humber, swallowed by the sea about 1350, or it may have belonged to some more ancient harbour which has sheltered the Dragons and Long-serpents of the northern Jarls.

Eaton Hall, Retford   John Cordeaux

(Lincolnshire Notes & Queries, Volume iii, No 20, October 1892)

Although I do not agree with his final conclusion that the site of Ravenser Odd, in its entirety, lies to the east of the present Spurn Point, his research into this anomaly is enlightening. Cordeaux's observation that the town might lie under, and through, the current peninsula is nearer the mark. Only further research will reveal whether there is any substance in his claims about the stone ridge to the east of Spurn. However, one tantalising possibility is that the bench is actually an artificial shelf, placed next to timber staithes so that ships at low tide could rest on them. As it appears that Hull had this arrangement in the 14th century, it is very likely that the contemporaneous port of Ravenser also used this method of construction. (Changing Faces, Watkin & Whitwell, diagram p52) If this proves to be the case, then the ridge, three quarters of a mile north of the lighthouse on the sea side, could be part of the harbour wall in the town. Incidentally, Angell's lighthouse of 1674 was on the seaward side of the Chalk Bank near this location, probably on a site on the lower beach. Smeaton, the architect of the lighthouse before the present one, placed it 1860 yards north of his 1776 built lighthouse. That is, just over a mile north of his lighthouse, which existed a few yards south of the present one built by Thomas Matthew. This exact location seems to have a very long history.

As recent research postulates the presence of two ridges in the location, one near the Binks, and one near the northern edge of the Chalk Bank, I feel that the track of this northern one could represent the shape of the promontory at the time of Ravenser and is roughly in the right location. There is support for this hypothesis from the Spurn Heritage Coast Study of 1992;

'The position of Ravenser Odd was at the point of Spurn, which according to De Boer's calculations from Meaux Chronicle records, lay approximately at the position of the present Chalk Bank. This implies that the point lay some 2.5 km north of its present position and over the location of the inner till ridge.' (IECS p21)

The coast was obviously much further to the east at Kilnsea, perhaps as much as a mile. The 'beak' of the 13th century point was not far from Old Kilnsea, and immediately south of this land tip was a cobble ridge, probably a glacial moraine which had been supplemented by gravel heaped up by the action of longshore drift, the one described in the original account;

'For access to which from ancient time from Ald Ravensere, a sandy road extended, covered with round and yellow stones, thrown up in a little time by the height of the floods, having a breadth which an archer can scarcely shoot across' (LTH p11, CM ii p121 - 122)

This is further supported by the above report of 1992:

'It seems probable that these gravels were bull-dozed inshore as the sea level rose during the early Holocene….. Aeolian (wind blown) processes would then have begun to form dunes on the highest gravel ridges which were the inner ridges and the Old Den. Thus a proto-Spurn would have consisted of an island, over the portion now marked by the Chalk Bank, connected to the mainland by an inter-tidal gravel beach.' (IECS p19)

With the aid of a modern aerial photograph (see the image on the front cover of the book) taken at low tide, one can trace out the line of this earlier promontory from the 'Old Den', the black shingle bank on the west, through the point at the north end of the Chalk Bank, to the shoals stretching away to the north east on the seaward side. Incidentally, the reference to an archer suggests that the path was quite wide, at least 200 yards or probably much more.

The devastating breach on Spurn Point in December 1849 occurred, according to Captain Vetch, who produced a report on the matter, about half a mile north of the lighthouse. This is close to the area where I believe the cobble road to Ravenser existed. Are the breach and the location of the cobble road connected? I believe that the testimony of two local people in his report is conclusive. Michael Tiddy, a coastguard, stated 'during the time of his occupation he has observed that stones and cobbles have been gathered from the shore where the breach is now made'. Another witness at the 1850 enquiry, John Barnby, assistant lighthouse keeper for 22 years, concurred, 'During his residence a quantity of cobble stones have been removed from the site of the breach' (DDCC / 89 / 97). During the 18th and 19th centuries, considerable quantities of shingle and cobbles were removed from Kilnsea and Spurn. Some was for ballast in ships, but later on, most was for constructing buildings or making toll roads. To further emphasise this, up to 45,000 tons per year were removed from the peninsula in the years 1800 to 1849. This amounts to in excess of one million tons of cobbles and gravel being removed in this period! (Mathison, The Spurn Gravel Trade p4) How serious this exploitation was is reinforced by the following statement, from William Shelford's work, 'Inhabitants of this district took, he might almost say, every particle of shingle they could catch. He had seen them even raking out the tide pools on the beach to get the shingle.' (SOH p32) No cobble bank could survive such an onslaught. The road to Ravenser was literally being removed, stone by stone, on an industrial scale in the 18th and 19th century.

In conclusion, I consider that the extreme tip of Ravenser Odd was on the site of the Old Den, and that the wharves, warehouses and premises led over Greedy Gut towards the present Spurn Point. The cobble road probably started under the current spit at the northern end of the Chalk Bank, and continued out to sea easterly, before curving north easterly and then northwards towards Old Kilnsea, the site of which is now far offshore under the restless waters of the North Sea.

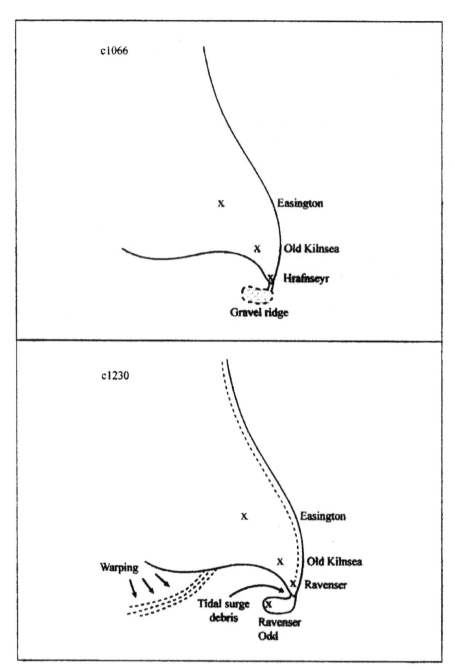

The top map illustrates how I believe the area looked c1066. Both Easington and Old Kilnsea were then considerably further from the sea. The gravel ridge consists of the glacial moraine left from the last ice age. The lower map illustrates the silting up (warping) of the estuary at that time. The gravel ridge is now connected to the mainland by sandbanks extending south from Old Ravenser and an accumulation of tidal debris. The dotted line is the coast in 1230, advancing on Old Kilnsea. (Maps not to scale)

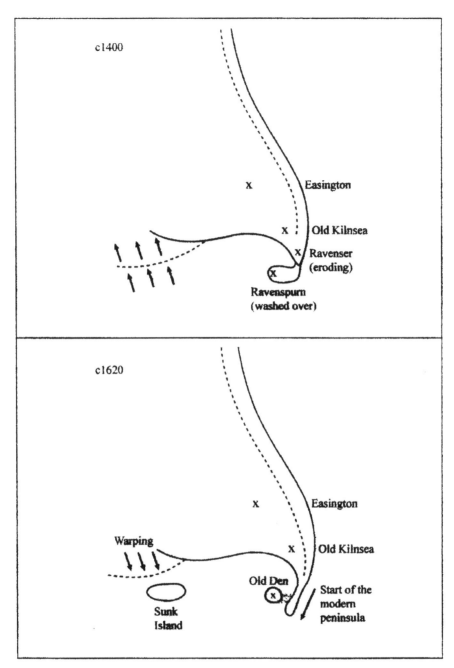

The dotted line in the upper map of 1400 illustrates the coastal erosion since 1066. The part of the ridge where Ravenser Odd was has now been washed over. The site has become known as Ravenspurn. The Humber is advancing back into previously silted up land and villages are being lost. The 1620 map shows the formation of the Old Den, as the former site of Ravenspurn detaches from the sand spit advancing past it. Warping once again is taking place, and Sunk Island has started to form. (Maps not to scale)

Ravenser Odds and ends!

There are a number of references and items relevant to Ravenser that do not readily fit into the chapter headings. I have taken the liberty of including them here in this mischievously named chapter!

While reading George De Boer's correspondence in the Hull History Centre, I came across a poem simply entitled 'Ravenser', and sent to him in 1961 by a certain Claire Ellin of Kilnwick (UDDB / 4 / 3 / 8)

The following published fiction books mention the place;

Paul Borquin (real name Richard Amberley) – 'The Lord of the Ravens', a tale of the life of the town and piracy, Faber 1961
Tessa Potter - Dark Waters, collection of short stories, Spindlewood, Barnstaple, 1995. 'The Flight from Odd' relates to the fate of a young monk at the time of its inundation.
Phil Mathison - On Macabre Lines, collection of short stories, Dead Good Publications, 2013. 'Beyond the end of the line' is a supernatural tale of the washing away of the bodies from the chapel.

Here are the well known references to the town in three of Shakespeare's plays;

Spoken by the Earl of Northumberland in Richard II, Act 2, Scene 1, lines 294 - 298
'Wipe off the dust that hides our sceptre's gilt,
And make high majesty look like itself,
Away with me in post to Ravenspurg;
But if you faint, as fearing to do so,
Stay and be secret, and myself will go.'

Spoken by Green in Richard II, Act 2, Scene 2, lines 49 – 51
'The banish'd Bolingbroke repeals himself,

And with uplifted arms is safe arrived
At Ravenspurg.'

Spoken by the Earl of Northumberland in Richard II, Act 2, Scene 3, lines 8 – 10
'But, I bethink me, what a weary way
From Ravenspurg to Cotswold will be found
In Ross and Willoughby, wanting your company.'

Spoken by Harry Percy in Richard II, Act 2, Scene 3, lines 30 - 35
'Because your lordship was proclaimed traitor.
But he, my lord, is gone to Ravenspurg,
To offer service to the Duke of Bedford,
And sent me over by Berkley, to discover
What power the Duke of York had levied there;
Then with direction to repair to Ravenspurg.'

Spoken by Hotspur in Henry IV Part 1, Act 1, Scene 3, lines 246 - 249
'His uncle York – where I first bow'd my knee
Unto this king of smiles, this Bolingbroke,
'Sblood!
When you and he came back from Ravenspurg.'

Spoken by King Henry in Henry IV Part 1, Act 3, Scene 2, lines 94 - 96
'For all the world,
As thou art to this hour, was Richard then,
When I from France set foot at Ravenspurg.'

Spoken by Hotspur in Henry IV Part 1, Act 4, Scene 3, lines 74 - 77
'He presently, as greatness knows itself,
Steps me a little higher than his vow
Made to my father, while his blood was poor,
Upon the naked shore at Ravenspurg.'

Spoken by King Edward in Henry VI Part 3, Act 4, Scene 7, lines 6 - 9
'And brought desired help from Burgundy;
What then remains, we being thus arriv'd
From Ravenspurg haven before the gates of York,
But that we enter, as into our dukedom?'

Additionally, there are at least two pieces of music that allude to the port;
Phil Mathison – 'The Legend of Ravenser', 2010, track available CD Baby www.cdbaby.com
Paul Davenport – 'Ravenser Odd' on the album 'Wait for no man', Hallamshire Traditions 2011 www.hallamtrads.co.uk

The town obviously lives on in the pages of the Meaux Chronicle, but there is something more tangible of the town in the thoroughfare called Ravenspurn Road at Patrington Haven, and a hostelry down Southcoates Lane in Hull called the Ravenser Hotel. Additionally, the family name of De-la-Pole, famous in Hull, originates from William and Richard De-la-Pole, merchants of Ravenser, who left the port in 1336.

As we have read in a previous chapter, one church bell from the chapel at Odd is reputed to have gone to All Saints church at Easington and two small ones are supposed to have been acquired by St. Bartholomew's church at Aldbrough, but there is no means of ascertaining if they survive at these locations.

Finally, no mention of the town would be complete without mentioning the Kilnsea cross, which is reputed to have come from Ravenspurn. Legend has it that the cross was erected to commemorate the landing of Henry, duke of Lancaster in 1399. It was moved in the early 19th century when Old Kilnsea was destroyed. Initially it went to Burton Constable for a short time, before ending up at Holyrood House, Hedon. The cross has some interesting images on its head (see rear cover of the book). One of the shields on the cross displays the coat of arms of the Nevil family of Westmorland. He was a prominent supporter of Henry of Lancaster IV, and this adds credence to the possibility that the cross originated at the site of the future king's landing place. (Gordon Ostler – Lost villages of the Humber Estuary p10)

Bibliography

Beresford, M W – The Lost Villages of Yorkshire (Part 2), Yorkshire Archaeological Journal XXXVIII 1952 – 5

Beresford, M W – History on the Ground, Methuen & Co 1957

Beresford, Maurice – New Towns of the Middle Ages, Lutterworth Press 1967

Beverley Treasure House – DDCC / 41 / 3, DDCC / 89 / 97, DDHI / 37, JL / 126 / 10

Blok, Petrus Johannes – History of the People of the Netherlands, G.P. Putnams & Son 1898

Boyle, J R – The Lost Towns of the Humber, A Brown & Sons, Hull & London 1889

De Boer, George – Spurn Head : Its History and Evolution, Institute of British Geographers, Transactions & Papers Publication No 34 1964

De Boer, George & Carr, A P – Early maps as historical evidence for coastal change, The Geographical Journal, Vol 135, Part 1, 3 / 1969

Dyson, Brian – A Guide to Local Studies in East Yorkshire, Hutton Press 1985

English, Barbara –The Lords of Holderness 1086 – 1260, Hull University Press 1991

Frost, Charles – Notices relative to the early history of the town and port of Hull, J B Nichols, London 1827

Hey, David – A Regional History of England : Yorkshire from AD 1000, Longman London 1986

Horrox, Rosemary (translated and edited) – The Black Death, Manchester University Press 1994

Hudson, Rev J Clare & Sympson, E Mansel (editors) - Lincolnshire Notes & Queries periodical

Hull History Centre – UDCC / 1 / 33, UDCC / 2 / 5, UDCC / 2 / 8, UDCC / 2 / 9, UDCC / 2 / 32, UDCC / 2 / 41, UDDB / 3 / 1 / 7, UDDB / 3 / 3 / 3, UDDB / 3 / 7 / 19, UDDB / 4 / 3 / 8, UDDB / 4 / 4 / 4

Kropf, L L – Spurnhead, the Early History of; In Page, W B (editor) – Hull & East Riding Portfolio, Volume 3 1887

Lamb, Hubert – Climate History & The Modern World, Routledge 2nd edition 1995

Lewis, David B (edited) – The Yorkshire Coast, Normandy Press 1991

Lloyd, T H – England and the German Hanse 1157 – 1611, A study of their Trade & Commercial Diplomacy, Cambridge University Press 1991

Mathison, P – The Spurn Gravel Trade, Dead Good Publications 2008

May, V J – Spurn Head, Extract from the Geological Conservation Review, Volume 28 2007

Miles, G T J & Richardson, W – The History of Withernsea, A Brown & Sons Ltd, Hull 1911

Morris, Collin – The Ravenser Composition, Proceedings of the Lincolnshire Architectural and Archaelogy Society, Volume 10, Part 1, 1963, p24 - 39

Neave, Susan & Ellis, Stephen – An Historical Atlas of East Yorkshire, University of Hull Press 1996

Ostler, Gordon – Lost Villages of the Humber Estuary, Local History Archives Unit 1990

Pye, Kenneth & Blott, Simon J – Aldbrough Gas Storage Project: Geomorphological assessment of impact of proposed cliff protection works on adjoining areas, External Investigation Report October 2010

Poulson, George – The History and Antiquities of the Seigniory of Holderness, Robert Brown, Hull 1840

Rawnsley, John E – Antique Maps of Yorkshire and Their Makers, M.T.D. Rigg Publications, 3rd edition 1983

Shelford, William – On the Outfall of the River Humber, edited James Forrest, William Clowes & Son, London 1869

Sheppard, Thomas – The Lost Towns of The Yorkshire Coast, A Brown & Sons, Hull & London 1912

Smeaton, John – A Narrative of the building and description of the construction of the Eddystone Lighthouse with stone: To which is subjoined an appendix giving some account of the lighthouse on the Spurn Point, built upon a sand, Longman, Hurst, Rees, Orme and Brown, 2nd edition 1813

Spurn Heritage Coast Study – Final report, Institute of Estuarine and Coastal Studies, University of Hull, January 1992

Tatchell, Molly – Ravenser Odd, Lost Port of the Humber, Unpublished document 1994, Local History Library, Grimsby and also Hull

Thompson, Thomas – Ocellum Promontorium, or short Observations on the Ancient State of Holderness with Historic Facts relative to the Sea Port & Market Town of Ravenspurn in Holderness, Thomas Tipping, Hull & London 1824

Victoria History of the Counties of England, Volume 1 1969 edited R.B. Pugh, Volume 5 1984 edited C R Elrington

Watkin, J R & Whitwell, J B – Changing Faces, Man in Humberside from the Stone Age to AD 1500, Humberside Heritage Publication No 9, 1987

Zimmern, Helen – The Hansa Towns, T Fisher, London 1889

Lightning Source UK Ltd.
Milton Keynes UK
UKOW05f2204211015

261124UK00001B/1/P